# What's Right for Me?

# Also for Teens from the Boys Town Press

*A Good Friend: How to Make One, How to Be One*

*Who's in the Mirror: Finding the Real Me*

*Boundaries: A Guide for Teens*

*Unmasking Sexual Con Games: A Teen's Guide to Avoiding Emotional Grooming and Dating Violence*

*Little Sisters, Listen Up!*

*Guys, Let's Keep It Real!*

## For a Boys Town Press catalog, call
# 1-800-282-6657

The Boys Town Press is the publishing division of Girls and Boys Town, the original Father Flanagan's Boys' Home.

# What's Right for Me?

## Making Good Choices in Relationships

Ron Herron
Val J. Peter

BOYS
TOWN
PRESS

BOYS TOWN, NEBRASKA

# What's Right for Me?

Published by The Boys Town Press
Father Flanagan's Boys' Home
Boys Town, Nebraska 68010

## Publisher's Cataloging in Publication

*(Prepared by Quality Books Inc.)*

Herron, Ronald W.
    Teens and relationships/by Ron Herron, Val J. Peter. –
1st ed.
    p. cm.
    LCCN:
    ISBN-13: 978-1-889322-19-3 (v.1) (pbk.)
    ISBN-10: 1-889322-19-9 (v.1) (pbk.)
    ISBN: 1-889322-20-2 (v.2)
    ISBN-13: 978-1-889322-21-6 (v.3) (pbk.)
    ISBN-10: 1-889322-21-0 (v.3) (pbk.)

    CONTENTS: v. 1. A good friend: how to make one, how to be one – v. 2. Who's in the mirror?: finding the real me – v. 3. What's right for me?: making good choices in relationships.
    SUMMARY: Teaches teens skills to enable them to develop self-esteem and healthy relationships with adults and other young people.
    1. Teenagers–Conduct of life. 2. Interpersonal relations in adolescence. I. Peter, Val. J. II. Father Flanagan's Boys' Home. III. Title. IV. Title: Good friend V. Title: Who's in the mirror VI. Title: What's right for me

BJ1661.H47 1998                158.1'0835
                               QBI98–117

10   9   8   7   6   5   4   3   2

▼ Teens who are having problems with
● relationships, drugs or alcohol use,
depression, parental conflict, or any other
kind of trouble, can call the **Girls and Boys
Town National Hotline, 1-800-448-3000,**
for help at any time.

▼ Italicized quotes are excerpted from
● "Ginger Snaps," 1976, and "The Spice of
Life," 1971, compiled by Dian Ritter, and
published by C.R. Gibson, Norwalk, CT.

# Table of Contents

# Introduction

The moon has a light side and a dark side. Things on the light side are clear and easy to see. Things on the dark side are unknown and hidden. People also can possess these traits. This book deals with the dark side of relationships.

The other two books in this series concerned friendship and self-improvement. They are valuable tools for creating healthy relationships. This book concentrates on coping with some of the unhealthy influences on teenage lives.

Growing up isn't easy. Although there are wonderful times ahead for you, there also will be some hurt and suffering. That is part of the human condition; no one escapes it. You have to play the cards life deals you. You have to make the most of the opportunities that come along as well as overcome or sidestep the obstacles.

To some teenagers, the words, "don't do that," are an invitation to do just the opposite. You

1

probably have many people in your life telling you what you shouldn't do. Sometimes you don't get any reasons – just, "don't do that."

You deserve an explanation. You also deserve to hear what you should do instead. That's the purpose of this book. It offers tips and suggestions to help you avoid the potholes scattered along the road to adulthood.

Consider this book to be like a driver's manual. Both give you guidelines and rules to live by in order to make safe journeys. This means watching out for others as well as yourself, and preparing yourself for hazardous conditions.

But just like a driver's manual, this is only a book. No one can make you read it or force you to do what it says. You have to drive the car and take the test. You can drive recklessly or you can drive safely. You can speed along without thinking about the limits that have been set for you or you can follow the rules. It's up to you.

There are many teenagers who think they don't have many choices. They believe their lives are completely ruled by adults. That's not true. First, there is no such thing as total independence. All of us have to depend on others. We are expected to play by the rules and abide by the laws set down for us. If we all did what we wanted when we wanted, we would have chaos.

Second, you are now at an age where you can begin to take charge of your life. Everything you have experienced can now be used to make good choices about how you are going to live your life. This is the beginning of an exciting journey to adulthood. But it takes effort. Most people want success; however, not all of them want it enough to work for it.

Do you have enough courage to meet life's challenges head-on? Are you going to charge ahead or retreat? It's your choice. You can learn new things that will help you take control of what happens to you, or you can sit back and let others call the shots. If you choose to do nothing, then it is true that adults and others around you will play a big role in determining your future.

Improving your life means continually learning new skills. There are no perfect answers. You can turn to those you love and trust for help and guidance. But your life is your life and no one else's; many times, you'll have to find your own way. Read this information as if you were eating a good meal. Chew it carefully and let it digest. It really is "food for thought."

This book also contains personal stories about teenagers who have made some mistakes. As you read their stories, their mistakes might be obvious to you. If they aren't, perhaps you can learn something that will help you recognize similar problems when they pop up in your life. The dark side of a personality or a relationship isn't easy to see unless you look carefully.

Each problem area was chosen because it affects every teenager's growth and development. Some of the problems may be big issues in your life; some may not. Some problems may be easily solved ; some may not. But all of them are real problems to look at and think about. There will be times when you will handle problems well and other times when you won't. There are some chances that are worth taking and there are some that are not. The information contained in this book will help you make the right decisions.

You might think that some of the information comes on too strongly. You may not like to read it. At times, you may think it's the same old song and dance you've heard from other adults. Maybe so. But the advice contained in each chapter has helped hundreds of teenagers solve their problems and go on to live happy lives.

So there's the sales pitch. Read on. We hope you learn something that will help you. Being a teenager can be fresh and exhilarating, but it can be spoiled very quickly by poor choices.

Now is the time to start taking responsibility for your life by making good decisions. Good luck.

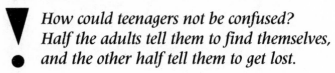

*How could teenagers not be confused?*
*Half the adults tell them to find themselves,*
*and the other half tell them to get lost.*

# Boundaries

Imagine riding alone in an elevator. You're free to move around as you like. You can sing, hum, or get lost in your thoughts. Then on the control panel, you see those little lights that indicate other people want to get on. Sure enough, when the elevator stops, new riders get on. Now you don't feel as comfortable as before, and you're maybe even a little self-conscious about being around a bunch of strangers. More people squeeze in and get closer and closer to you. Now you're feeling crowded. Someone with a cold begins sneezing and coughing. Soon the elevator is stuffed with people. Some look surly and unhappy. Someone steps on your foot; then you're pushed and scrunched against the wall. You smell someone's breath and body odor. Yuck! You can't wait to get out of there. You no longer feel at ease; you feel trapped.

This example illustrates boundaries – the personal space that you keep between yourself and others. There are two general types of boundaries you should be aware of:

**Physical** – These boundaries protect your body. You decide who can touch you, how they can touch you, and so on. Physical boundaries include sexual areas.

**Emotional** – These boundaries protect your thoughts and emotions. You decide what feelings you will or will not share with others.

Boundaries are important because they define areas where you feel secure and worthwhile. A boundary is a physical or emotional "comfort zone."

## ⊩ Marcie's Story

*Marcie always worried about how other people felt. She had been a "people pleaser" since she was a little girl. Now that she was older, she often thought of becoming a nurse.*

*Marcie first met Brian in the guidance counselor's office. She was switching classes to acquire a study hall at the end of the day. His family had just moved in from New York, and he and the counselor were arranging his class schedule. Marcie and Brian finished working on their schedules at the same time. She asked him what he thought of the town and if he had any brothers and sisters, and they made the usual small talk for about five minutes.*

*As it turned out, they were in two of the same classes. Brian was talkative and asked questions all the time. They started eating lunch and study- ing for tests together. He talked about what it was like growing up in New York City, about his screwed-up family, his old girlfriend who broke his heart, the time he thought about committing suicide because of her, and the times he saw his dad beat his mom. These things disturbed Marcie, and she felt so sorry for him that she almost cried.*

*After the first few weeks of school, Brian started passing notes to Marcie after class. Soon the notes started to bother Marcie. They were too personal, and she noticed that Brian was becom- ing a little too friendly when they were talking. She had made it very clear that friendship was the only thing on her mind and that she didn't want to date Brian. But that didn't stop Brian from continually asking personal questions: What did she wear to bed – a nightgown or pajamas? What was her bra size? What did she think was sexy about the guys she knew? What kinds of things "turned her on?"*

*Marcie was in a bind. She didn't want to hurt Brian's feelings because she knew he was really sensitive. But she hated those questions, and they made her uncomfortable. She tried to tell Brian*

7

*in a nice way to stop it, but he just didn't get the hint. She finally decided that she had to tell him to quit asking her such personal questions.*

*The next day when they were eating lunch together, Brian began asking questions again. Marcie thought this was the perfect time to tell him what she was feeling. She said, "You know Brian, we've done a lot of stuff together. . .," and he interrupted her: "You're gonna dump me, aren't you?" He had a hurt look on his face that upset her. She took a deep breath and said, "Well, no, not really. I just thought that some of the things you've been talking about lately have made me kind of uncomfortable."*

*Whew. She had said it. Marcie had always had trouble saying anything that she thought might hurt someone. She usually hedged instead of telling someone the straight truth. Brian wrinkled his face quizzically and said, "Like what?" Marcie told him that she didn't like talking about personal and private things and then she gave him some examples. She said she didn't like being asked questions about sex and what she wore to bed and things like that.*

*He hung his head and said, "I wish you'd have said something earlier. I didn't think you minded anything we talked about. I just wanted to get to know you. We could've talked about something else."*

*Marcie realized that she should have been up front with Brian from the beginning. She realized that she needed to work on setting limits and letting people know exactly what those limits were. And it was clear that Brian just didn't have a clue about the things girls wanted to talk about. It had always been a struggle for him to fit in with other kids. He just tried too hard. When his girlfriend dumped him (she was his girlfriend in his mind, though not hers), he blamed himself for being so terrible at relationships. He thought he needed to talk aggressively about sex like some of the "jocks" did. It seemed to work for them. He really didn't know what was appropriate and what wasn't, what he should or shouldn't say. He was just guessing.*

*Marcie and Brian made a deal that day: Anytime he said or did something to make her uncomfortable, she would say "Red light," and he would stop whatever he was doing. Gradually, Brian learned more about personal boundaries, and Marcie learned to be more open and assertive. They are still close friends.*

If you recognized that Brian was saying things that offended or embarrassed Marcie, good for you. You have an accurate picture of what personal boundaries are. And if you knew that Marcie should have said something earlier, you understand how important it is to let people know what those boundaries are. It's not impolite

or unreasonable to say "stop," whenever someone makes you feel uncomfortable.

When people cross a boundary you have set,
it should make you uneasy. Think of your own
experiences. Has a stranger ever stood so close
to you that you were nervous? Has anyone ever
touched you in a way that was "overly friendly?"
Did someone you didn't know very well ever
sneak up behind you and pinch or grab you, or
start rubbing your shoulders? Has anyone ever
asked very personal questions that embarrassed
or upset you? Those are all boundary issues.
Those people were just "too close for comfort."

It's important for people to know what you
stand for. It's equally important that they know
what you won't stand for.

To understand boundaries better, imagine a
series of invisible rings that start to go around you
close to your body, then gradually spread out.
They resemble the ripples a stone makes when
it's tossed in the water. Some rings are close; others are farther away. These rings represent how
physically close you will let people be to you and
determine how many of your personal thoughts
you will share with them.

Everyone you encounter fits somewhere in
these boundary lines. Strangers are the farthest
away, with casual acquaintances a little closer,

and good friends and family in the inner circles, closest to you.

## How Boundaries Affect Your Life

Think of something you do or say that your friends kid you about in a good-natured way. Now imagine that a stranger tried to make the same joke. You'd probably be offended or angry. That is because your friends have shared experiences with you, so they fit in one of your closer boundaries. The stranger does not.

What about relationships with members of the opposite sex? People can step over the line of personal boundaries. Girls are often the targets of guys who come on too strong. These guys try to go too far too soon with touching, kissing, or even conversation. Dates become wrestling matches. Unfortunately, some guys view girls as objects of desire instead of human beings who deserve to be treated with respect. They are violating the girls' physical and emotional boundaries.

That's why girls need to set limits and let boys know what those limits are. At times, they will need to say firmly, "Don't do that," or "You're getting too close." Guys need to respect and honor those boundaries.

Guys can have their boundaries violated, too. A boy could go out with a girl who wants to get serious right away. She might want him to be with her all the time and not hang out with his friends anymore. She might send him letters saying she would "die" without him, tell other kids how much in love they are, telephone him at all hours of the day and night, or give him presents that he doesn't want. She might smother him with attention that embarrasses him. She is trying to get closer than he wants her to be.

Think of a boundary as a comfort zone. When you feel uncomfortable with what a person says or does, it is likely that that person crossed a personal boundary. Realize that you have the right to tell someone "no" when you feel that your boundaries have been crossed.

 *It's amazing how many things people turn on and off during the day – including people.*

## Sexual Boundaries

During the teenage years, sexual boundaries are particularly important. They develop and change as you mature. For example, when a two-year-old boy kisses a two-year-old girl, everyone thinks it's cute. It's a sign of friendship. But when the same boy and girl are 16 and start kissing, the relationship takes on a new meaning.

How you touch others and how they touch you are boundary issues. There is appropriate touch – a handshake, a pat on the back, slapping "high fives" – that people use as a sign of friendship. This type of touch is nonsexual and is used to show respect, excitement, teamwork, and so on. Another type of touch is sexual in nature – kissing, caressing. These are the ways people in a loving relationship show affection.

In dating relationships, sexual touching should progress gradually and have limits. But this is an area where many teens have boundary problems. Some find themselves struggling with an intimate relationship because they set inappropriate boundaries or set no boundaries at all. In the process, they are setting themselves up for problems they aren't emotionally ready to handle. Teenagers who don't understand what an appropriate boundary is also run the risk of being sexually and emotionally used and abused.

People who want you to go from saying "hi" to having sex aren't concerned about you or your feelings. Neither are people who try to trick you or gradually talk you into a sexual relationship. Anyone who uses you will try to convince you that they care, but they really are exploiting you. They are trying to leap from your farthest boundary to your closest. They have selfish motives. Don't allow anyone to trick or hurry you into sex. It is not right, and you are not emotionally ready for the responsibilities that go with a sexual relationship. Protect your sexual boundaries and your emotional boundaries as well.

## How Do People Violate Boundaries?

These behaviors are violations of your boundaries:

✔ Butting in on a conversation when you are talking to someone else.

✔ Stealing something of yours.

✔ Cruelly teasing or making fun of you, especially in front of others.

✔ Asking very personal questions.

✔ Touching your shoulder or leg, or another part of your body.

✔ Trying to "brainwash" you into doing something wrong.

✔ Sharing private information about you with other people.

✔ Making you feel uncomfortable by invading your "private space."

✔ Saying or doing things in front of you that you find offensive or gross.

✔ Always trying to sit or stand next to you.

✔ Forcing you to do something sexual.

✔ Physically or sexually abusing you.

# Unhealthy Boundaries

Healthy boundaries protect a person's body, thoughts, and feelings. On the other hand, having unhealthy boundaries makes you physically and emotionally vulnerable, and can lead to dangerous situations.

Unfortunately, some people have a problem knowing what "normal" is. They may come from a family that doesn't provide good role models for them. A traumatic event in their lives may have jarred their emotional compass, so their relationships with others are "all-or-nothing" affairs.

Here are some characteristics of unhealthy boundaries:

## Too Rigid

✔ Not allowing anyone to get close

✔ Difficulty in choosing and keeping friends

✔ Withdrawing and rejecting attempts by others to be friends

✔ Being isolated from others

✔ Never talking about personal feelings

## Too Loose

✔ Displaying inappropriate affection (clinging, pawing, suggestive language)

✔ Always doing what others say; never disagreeing or saying "no"

✔ Saying or doing sexually suggestive things in front of others

✔ Sharing personal information with anyone who will listen

✔ Having many sexual experiences

## Setting Healthy Boundaries

Here are some ways to set appropriate boundaries:

✔ Identify trustworthy peers, and make friends with them.

✔ Learn to identify and avoid people who look out only for their own interests.

✔ Speak up when someone or something bothers you. Let people know what you won't tolerate.

✔ Spend time with people you enjoy being with and who aren't just looking for something from you in return.

✔ Define your boundaries with others. Share personal thoughts only with people you trust. Learn to say "no" to negative peer pressure.

✔ Trust your feelings of comfort or discomfort. These are good indicators of right and wrong.

✔ Learn to look at problems objectively. Think of various options and what might happen with each one. Make a plan to solve the problem; then go for it.

✔ Identify situations in which your boundaries have been violated in the past. Determine how you will handle similar situations in the future.

✔ Talk with a trusted adult or close friend about your boundaries and ask whether he or she thinks they are healthy. Get advice about how to improve them.

If a person always makes you uncomfortable, you need to tell the person how you feel. It's possible that he or she can change. On the other hand, if your feelings go beyond just feeling uncomfortable and you feel nervous and maybe even a little afraid, talk to a trusted adult and ask for help.

Once you set healthy boundaries, you will feel much better about yourself and you will be proud of yourself for doing the right thing. When you have clearly defined your boundaries, it becomes easier for other people to recognize them. Saying, "I don't like that," "I'm not comfortable doing that," or "I'm sorry, that's not for me," is a simple way to let others know what boundaries you have set for yourself.

▼  *A man can stand a lot as long as he can*
●  *stand himself.*

## Sharing Your Thoughts with Others

How much do you tell others about yourself? Would you describe yourself as talkative or quiet? Funny or serious? Carefree or inhibited? What words do you think other people would use to describe you?

An important part of your relationships with other people is how much you let them see into your life. Sharing your feelings and talents is crucial to a friendship. But in the beginning stages of a relationship, how much personal information should you share?

Sharing personal thoughts with others can be scary. You always run the risk of feeling rejected or being made fun of if you say the wrong things. Or the person with whom you shared your personal thoughts could tell others.

Maybe you know people who tell you too much about themselves and their feelings. It makes you uncomfortable, doesn't it? Every sordid detail is vividly laid out for you. People who "bare their souls" to anyone who will listen have boundaries that are too loose.

On the other hand, people who don't share anything about themselves usually are not very well-liked. They appear cold and unfeeling. There might be valid reasons for not disclosing any personal information, but it doesn't help them develop relationships. It's unhealthy for people to hide all of their feelings and never share them with anybody. These are boundaries that are too rigid.

So, what are you supposed to do? If you never reveal any of your emotions – if you have very strict boundaries – people may think you're cold. If you tell everything about yourself – if you have very loose boundaries – people may think you're pushy.

The key is to find a comfort level with each person. You need to put people in the appropriate area of your boundaries. (Remember the "rings" we discussed earlier?)

Most of us share private information with our best friends and family. This includes feelings of happiness, loneliness, fear, pride, grief, and so on. The less familiar we are with someone, the less personal information we should share. For example, with people who are only acquaintances – classmates, kids we're in sports or other activities with, people we see every day but really aren't friends with – we tend to talk about things like the weather, sports, movies, and so on. And we exchange only as much information as we have to with strangers, such as sales clerks or the person sitting next to us on the bus.

Start out by sharing a little bit at a time. Don't tell your innermost thoughts, but don't keep everything locked up inside, either. Knowing what and how much to share will improve your relationships with others. They are more likely to view you as flexible, open, and nice to be around.

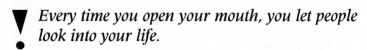 *Every time you open your mouth, you let people look into your life.*

Set healthy boundaries and stick with them. You'll protect yourself and be more likely to find someone who is good for you. And you will be good for that person in return. That's true friendship.

# Harmful
# or Violent
# Relationships

Relationships can be wonderful. But like anything else in life, some relationships don't work out as we would like. Not all relationships are healthy and constructive.

Sometimes it's hard to figure out who is good for us and who isn't. Some people play games. Others want control or just want to take, take, take, and never give of themselves. Some resort to manipulation, force, or intimidation to get what they want.

**▼** *We too often love things and use people when we*
**•** *should be using things and loving people.*

## ▌ Alexis' Story

*Alexis was thrilled when Damon first asked her out. He was cute and popular and had the sweetest smile. Damon was well-liked by most of*

21

*the kids in school. Alexis and Damon seemed like the perfect couple. The other girls envied her, and she loved it. She was on top of the world.*

*They hadn't dated long when Damon first said he was falling in love with her. He was so attentive; it was like he hung on every word she said. He drove her to school, ate lunch with her, took her home, called her. She loved it. She had finally found a guy who listened and who enjoyed being with her. Her whole life was revolving around someone who really cared for her.*

*Then it happened. One Friday night, they went to a party at his friend's house. She knew Damon had been drinking, but she didn't think he had had much. "He's not drunk or anything," she remembers thinking. When they got into the car, he told her to sit next to him. Since his car had bucket seats, Alexis didn't think that was a very good idea, and said, "That's all right, I'll just sit here." Damon told her again, and she said, "It's okay, all right. This seat is just fine." Suddenly, Damon exploded. He grabbed her left arm and shouted, "Don't argue with me. I said sit here, dammit!" Then he pulled her roughly onto the console. He said, "Look, you're my woman. And you know how much I care about you, so do what I say. I want everyone to see you sitting here. It ain't gonna kill you or anything, is it?"*

*He was slurring his words and she thought that he had drunk more than she had realized. Sitting on the console was really uncomfortable but she was afraid to move. She wondered what was wrong with him, and if she had said or done something to make him mad. Regardless, she wasn't going to make matters worse by saying anything now.*

*By the time they reached her house, Damon had calmed down. As she got out, he said, "Alexis, look, I'm sorry I yelled at you. Let's forget it, okay? I'll call you tomorrow."*

*Alexis felt better knowing that he had apologized. "He's just having a bad day, that's all," she thought.*

*But more bad days were in store. Damon became more and more controlling. He wanted her to be with him all the time. If they couldn't be together, he wanted to talk on the phone for long periods of time. Many times, she felt like they said the same things over and over. When they did go out, they went where he wanted to go. He was still nice, but his attentiveness now felt like possessiveness. He was very jealous and didn't want her to talk with any other guys unless he was around. She kept telling herself that his attention was just his way of showing how much he cared for her. She knew everything would get better with time.*

*Alexis didn't hang around with her girlfriends much anymore. She missed them. Once she over-heard one of them say, "She doesn't have time for us. She's too busy with Mr. Bigshot." That certain-ly wasn't true, and although Alexis wanted to tell them the truth, she just couldn't. She just slowly slipped away from most of them. Alexis didn't even tell her closest friend, Melissa, about Damon's possessiveness.*

*One night, Alexis and Damon went to a movie. As they were walking out, he told her that he had promised his buddies that he and Alexis would join them after the movie. Alexis said, "Damon, why do we have to be with your friends all the time? Can't we do something else?"*

*He just stood there and glared at her. As other people were coming out of the theater, he said sternly, "Get in the car." As she started to get in, Damon grabbed her arms, turned her around so that she faced him, shook her, and then pushed her in the car. He gritted his teeth and said, "Don't you ever argue with me when other people are around. I hate that!" His voice had a gravelly, growling sound like a wild dog. It scared her. He was still standing by the passenger door, and she could see him breathing heavily. His hands were shaking. She said, "Calm down, Damon. I didn't mean anything bad about your friends. I just thought. . ." His slap came out of nowhere. It felt like stinging bees had attacked her face. She was afraid. She began sobbing and saying she was sorry for making him mad. She begged him to forgive her. Her mind was reeling: "What did I do wrong? What caused him to do that?"*

*He got in on the driver's side. He hung his head and said, "I'm sorry, honey. I don't know what happened. I just lost it. It'll never happen again. I promise."*

*She wanted desperately to believe him.*

*The next day, he sent her flowers with a card that contained a famous poem, "How Do I Love Thee?" The other girls thought it was sweet. One girl cooed, "Oh, he's so thoughtful and sensitive."*

*"It won't happen again. It won't happen again." Alexis wondered how often she heard those words in the weeks since he had first slapped her. They soon had a hollow sound. His anger had gotten worse. She couldn't count the times he had slapped, grabbed, shaken, or yelled at her. Occasionally, she had welts and bruises on her arms that she covered up with long-sleeved blouses or sweaters. He always was sorry afterwards and usually bought her gifts to prove how much he cared. But the good times between his violence became shorter and shorter. And she never knew what was going to set him off next.*

*Alexis felt alone and scared. She knew she had to tell someone, but whom? Her parents would want to call the police or Damon's parents. Her dad would want to interrogate her and get the details. She knew it would be an ugly scene.*

*She didn't want to tell any of her old friends, either. Some of them wouldn't believe her. And there was a part of her that didn't want to destroy the image of Damon and her as "the perfect couple." It made her feel special that she had something someone else wanted. It was a stupid thought; she knew that. It was silly pride. But if she and Damon split up, it would seem as though she had failed somehow.*

*Alexis finally decided to call Melissa. She started out by saying, "Please do one thing for me. Just listen. Please promise me that you won't tell anyone or do anything. Okay?"*

*Melissa was the perfect person to talk with. She listened and comforted Alexis. She was a good friend, and Alexis felt safe and secure for the first time in a long time. One thing Melissa said really stuck with Alexis. It became a source of strength for her. She said, "You don't deserve this. You don't deserve to be abused."*

*The truth stunned her. Amid all of her other thoughts, she had denied the fact that Damon was abusive. She had been so caught up in her emo-*

*tions – the worrying, agony, stress – that she failed to see what was so obvious: She was being abused.*

*Alexis finally broke up with Damon. It was messy and painful and emotionally draining, but she knew she had to do it. Damon cried and pleaded with her, and vowed he would change if she'd just give him one more chance. There were moments when she wanted to give in. But she stuck with her decision. She had seen his remorse turn into anger and violence too many times before. When she felt like changing her mind, Melissa's words would come back to her and wrap her up like an old favorite blanket that kept her safe and warm: "You don't deserve this. You don't deserve to be abused."*

Alexis' story is like those of thousands of teenagers who have fallen into abusive dating relationships. And many stories are worse than hers. Most people don't want to admit they are in a harmful relationship. They want so desperately to believe that everything is okay that they don't see the truth. They are so trapped in the relationship that they can't see any way out.

Many people avoid the pain of a breakup by thinking that things will work out. It often seems too difficult to sort through the maze of emotions surrounding the relationship. The truth is, relationships can flourish, get boring, grow sour, or even become abusive. People have to work at getting along with others; there are no quick and easy ways, no shortcuts to healthy relationships.

The following questions will help you take a closer look at your friendships and dating relationships. If you answer "yes" to several questions, you're probably in an unhealthy relationship and need some help. Call a domestic violence hotline or talk to someone you can trust. The Boys Town National Hotline is an excellent resource. It handles close to half a million calls a year. Many of those calls are from teens about harmful relationships. The toll-free number is 1-800-448-3000.

## Relationships Questionnaire

1. Do I ever feel used or treated like an object?

2. Am I spending too much time thinking about the way I'm treated in this relationship?

3. Have I lost interest in things I used to like? Do I feel isolated from my old friends?

4. Do I ever feel I'm being intimidated or forced into doing something I don't want to do?

5. Am I embarrassed at things my friend does to me or with me? Am I made fun of or put down in front of others?

6. Have I ever felt unsafe or been afraid of what my friend might do to me?

7. Have I ever been threatened with words or physical force?

8. Has my friend ever forced or tried to force me into doing something sexual by threatening to end the relationship?

9. Does my friend ever get extremely mad at things, and I don't understand why? Does he or she take it out on me or others?

10. Does my friend make excuses for what he or she has done? Does my friend fail to realize that I was hurt? Do I get blamed for what happened?

11. Does my friend blame his or her violent behavior on alcohol or drugs?

12. Has my friend ever hit, slapped, pushed, or choked me?

# Danger Signs in Relationships

If you are in a relationship in which any of the following is taking place, the chances of having a positive relationship are slim. Get out of the relationship.

**1** **One-Sidedness** – One person dominates the relationship. Everything has to go his or her way. The friendship seems to hinge on whether he or she is happy. You only go where they want to go and do what they want to do.

**2** **Manipulation** – The person does anything to get what he or she wants. The person takes advantage of you for personal gain. This person tells lies or uses word games, and may resort to threats or intimidation.

**3** **Possessiveness** – The person becomes extremely jealous if you talk or hang around with other people. He or she has to have your loyalty and blind devotion. You are not supposed to give anyone else positive attention. If you're not with this person, he or she wants to know where you go, whom you are with, and what you are doing. Even your thoughts seem to be under investigation.

**4** **Unrealistic Demands** – The person tells you that you must think, act, or dress a certain way in order to remain friends. He or she tells you what you should believe or tries to convince you that others can't be trusted. Basically, the person says, "Do it my way or good-bye."

▼ *There can be no happiness in life if the things we*
● *believe in are different from the things we do.*

**5** **Anger** – The person gets extremely angry or violent. The person may threaten you, hit you, say nasty and cruel things, or use other force to keep you under control. When these things happen, or if you're ever worried about your safety, get out of the relationship quickly. If you don't, the anger and violence will only get worse and someone will get hurt. Go to someone you trust for help if you're worried that you can't handle it by yourself.

These are common signs of unhealthy relationships. They happen too frequently – even in marriages. When they do, the relationship continues to deteriorate. Healthy feelings can be smothered by one person's domination or demands.

It doesn't have to be that way. Look at your relationships objectively. Be honest with yourself. You have to step back and figure out what's wrong before you can fix it.

## How to Build Healthy Relationships

**1** **Take your time.** Really getting to know and trust someone occurs as you have many experiences together. Never rush into a relationship or allow someone to rush you. Take it slowly. If it is good, it will last.

31

**2** **Be sure your relationships involve an even give and take.** Look to see if there is a healthy balance. No person should control or do all of the taking. In other words, make sure you and your friends have the same expectations for your relationships. Let them know what you believe in and where you will draw the line.

**3** **Don't allow yourself to spend a great deal of time worrying about your relationships.** They are just one part of your life and they shouldn't monopolize your time. You have other responsibilities. Your friends should respect your desire to lead a balanced life.

It's okay to ask yourself questions and look at your own behavior as you attempt to solve problems. That's healthy. But that's entirely different from slacking off in school, at home, or on the job because you are constantly thinking about a relationship. Do the good things that are expected of you and good things will happen to you.

**4** **Realize that relationships constantly change.** And so will you. Learn how to adjust to these changes without giving up the things you enjoy and believe in.

**5** **Look at past relationships that were positive.** Think about what made them special. Then look at relationships that didn't work out. Although relationships are a two-way street, try to figure out what part you played in the way each relationship developed. Use what you learned to make a current relationship better.

**6** **Write down why certain people make good friends.** Look for those qualities in others.

**7** **Write down things people do that you don't like.** Steer clear of people who do these things.

If someone hits, slaps, or threatens you once in a relationship, it will happen again. Physical or emotional abuse has no place in a healthy relationship. Don't set yourself up to be hurt again.

Some relationships can't be fixed. If you aren't happy with a relationship now, take some time to ask yourself why. Then do something about the situation. Doing nothing will accomplish nothing, and the relationship will remain the same or get worse, not better.

Learn to be objective when you look at your relationships. Think about what happens as a result of being with someone. If you frequently get into trouble, feel taken for granted, or feel bad about your friends, you need to change something in the relationship or get out of it altogether. Learn to recognize people who don't have your best interests at heart so that you can avoid them. Take charge of your life. On the other hand, learn to recognize the qualities that make up a good relationship and work on keeping those relationships happy and healthy.

If you have questions about healthy relationships, please talk to a trusted adult. Talk to your parents, school counselor, or a teacher. They have experienced the good and the bad of relationships in their lives, too. They can help you head down the right path, a path that leads to good friends and fulfilling relationships.

# Jealousy and Envy

Jealousy can place a curse on relationships. It is an ugly, nagging feeling that brings out the worst in us. And jealousy can be a breeding ground for a whole band of other emotions that lead to negative behavior.

Before we look more closely at jealousy, let's take a look at its kid sister, envy. Both these emotions have plagued people for a long time. The Bible frequently mentions them. Shakespeare coined a phrase calling jealousy the "green-eyed monster." And it's often said that some people are "green with envy."

Let jealousy and envy run wild, and you've got major problems getting along with others. Letting them control your thoughts and behavior leads to unhappiness.

# Envy

Envy is a painful awareness of what someone else has, and wanting the same things. You might envy someone for having a nice car, a big house, good looks, or lots of money. You could envy someone for being popular, smart, or athletic. You might envy someone who doesn't have to work as hard or as much as you do. You might spend a lot of time daydreaming about what you'd be like if you had it so good.

You've probably felt something like this before, right? Envy makes you think that you're being treated unfairly. Other people always have something you don't have, or can do something you can't do. You may feel resentful, even angry, about how easy they have it. At the same time you curse your own bad luck.

How can you control envy? The first thing you must do is turn your head away and refuse to listen to it. Envy is a nasty, catty little troublemaker who likes to see people suffer. Realize that feeling sorry for yourself won't accomplish anything. Envy will make you dwell on your bad luck. If you listen, you'll end up feeling even worse.

Being mad at the other person won't accomplish anything, either. Being envious is a colossal waste of time. Stop yourself from wanting what someone else has. If there is a reasonable chance of earning or having whatever it is you're envious of, then go for it. Make a plan and stick with it. But if it's something that you can never have, turn your attention away from negative feelings and go after something you can achieve. Don't lose sight of the good things in your life and the talents that you already have.

It's best to get on with your life and do the things that you are supposed to do. Concentrate on doing the things that you do well. Appreciate what you have; don't feel bad about what you don't have. Focus your mind on becoming a better person. It's quite likely other kids will end up envying you!

 *When people turn green with envy, they are ripe for trouble.*

## Jealousy

Being jealous means you are afraid that another person is going to steal your special friend or loved one. Jealousy makes you fearful, angry, and worried. It makes you feel bitter, worthless, or rejected. These feelings can be very intense. Jealousy holds tremendous emotional power.

## ▌ Beth's Story

Joe and Beth met at the fast-food restaurant where they both had summer jobs and frequently worked the same weeknight shifts. After work, they rode around or went to a movie. On weekends, they usually planned a special outing. It didn't really matter what they did; they had fun just being together. They were never at a loss for something to say and often talked for hours at a time. Beth felt comfortable and secure when she was with Joe. In fact, she thought their relationship was turning from friendship into romance.

In the fall, Joe changed hours at the restaurant so he could work weekends and weekdays after school. He was in the class play and wanted to keep up with his studies, and working weeknights just didn't fit his schedule. Beth didn't like that at all. It seemed as though she hardly saw him. They still went out on weekends, but she wanted to see him more often than that. He called occasionally and they had friendly talks, but he always seemed too busy to talk with her now.

Beth had a lot of time to think about their relationship. None of the other guys she knew were as nice as Joe; he treated her with respect. Her two previous boyfriends lied to her and played mind games. They both trampled her emotions, and she was careful about getting hurt again. Joe was different; she knew she could trust him.

*A couple of the guys she worked with asked her out, but she refused. She knew no one could be as special to her as Joe was. In fact, not seeing him made her remember how great he was to her.*

*At some point, Beth's feelings took a nosedive. She began having these nagging feelings about Joe. She was lonely and missed him. It seemed to her that his play practices lasted a long time. And his grades were never that good before; he wasn't a genius or anything. When did he get so serious about school? She began thinking that those were pretty lame excuses for changing his work hours.*

*Then her mind took a detour. She wondered if he was lying to her and going out with someone else. She thought, "What girl in her right mind wouldn't want to go out with Joe? He's probably got them lined up waiting to date him."*

*This was a terrible thought. Could he be as sneaky and manipulative as her other boyfriends? Why did she always pick such losers? She felt she probably deserved it. She began thinking that Joe deceived her just as the other guys did. She thought about all the nice things he had said and done. "How stupid am I, anyway? He didn't mean any of it. He was just using me," she thought.*

*Beth convinced herself that Joe had found someone else; she knew that other girls were much prettier than she was. She should have known that it was only a matter of time until one latched on to him. The more she thought about it, the more vivid her imagination became. It was like a movie. She thought about him kissing and hugging someone else; she imagined him dancing closely, looking into some girl's eyes and smiling contentedly. Then she thought of him laughing whenever someone mentioned her name or asked about her. He would say, "Beth? Oh, what a loser. I dumped her a long time ago." It was painful to think about.*

*Beth's daydreams became more frequent. She started getting angry at the idea that Joe was lying to her. Then she would switch gears and feel sad and depressed because she was losing him. She felt powerless. Her mind kept racing and she would go from one emotion to another – sadness, anger, depression, worry, resentment. Her thoughts went round and round. She looked at her gerbil in his cage and thought her life was just like his – running around inside a plastic wheel and getting nowhere. It all seemed so hopeless and there was nothing she could do to change what was happening.*

*One day Beth made an excuse to skip work. She was going to see how long these play practices really lasted. She drove to Joe's school, parked in the lot, and waited in the car for an hour. A few kids straggled in and out, talking and laughing, but there was no sign of Joe. Every time someone would walk nearby, she would slide down in the seat so no one could see her. "This is so crazy," she thought to herself.*

*And then she saw him. It was dark but it was obvious that he was with two girls. They were walking to the parking lot. "If he gives one of them a ride, I'll just die," she thought. She decided to leave. Then she asked herself what in the world she was thinking. She couldn't quit. She couldn't give Joe up without a fight. She got out of her car and dashed over to where they were standing.*

*Joe must have seen the crazy look in her eyes because he didn't say anything; he only stared. Beth started screaming, "I knew you were going out with someone else! Why didn't you have guts enough to tell me? Don't I at least deserve a phone call?"*

*Joe was stunned. Beth stood there with tears streaming down her face. Joe finally said, "Beth, this is my cousin, Angela; she's in the play, too. And this is our new drama teacher, Mrs. Johnson."*

41

*Beth felt so humiliated. She ran crying to her car. Her jealousy had made her lose touch with what was real. She was embarrassed by the fact that her emotions had been so strong that they had caused her to do something so foolish.*

Jealousy has been a destructive force in many relationships. Just as in Beth's case, jealousy's pure emotional force can replace logical thinking.

Does this mean it's wrong to be jealous? Not necessarily. All of us would worry if we thought someone we care about was going to leave to be with someone else. But just like other negative feelings, if jealousy is not controlled or redirected, it can snuff out a relationship in no time. You can learn how to deal with jealousy just as you can learn how to deal with other problems. But first, let's look at what jealousy can do to us.

Jealousy can occur in friendships, dating relationships, and, unfortunately, even in marriages. Relationships are damaged when jealous behaviors get too intense. Jealous behaviors include being sarcastic, telling lies, trying to make a friend feel guilty, or checking out a friend's story to see if he or she is telling the truth. "Playing detective" – trying to find out exactly what the friend did, where, and with whom – shows that trust isn't a foundation of the friendship.

Sometimes people become depressed. They feel sorry for themselves and tell themselves that they didn't deserve to be treated well in the first place. Some people even go so far as to think or do self-destructive things. They think that, if nothing else, maybe other people will see how bad they feel and comfort them a little bit. They're asking for pity and sympathy for their failures at relationships.

It's easy to point fingers and say it was someone else's fault that a relationship failed. When jealousy takes over, you think the other person deserves to suffer as much as you. It's not the truth and it's not the right thing to do, but it's how you feel.

**!** *A rumor is about as hard to unspread as butter.*

Jealousy reaches its peak when people become violent. That's the darkest side. When extremely jealous people think that their friend or loved one is giving time and attention to someone else and not to them, they can resort to destructive acts. These acts are aimed at hurting someone, and can include intimidation, threats, or violence. If a person is drinking or taking drugs, these negative feelings may burn out of control, like a raging emotional fire. It's much more likely that people under the influence of alcohol or drugs will do something destructive.

**❢** *The best thing to do behind a person's back is to pat it.*

Many jealous people launch into fits of violent rage with no thought of what they are doing. Ironically, people who do this actually hurt the ones they say they love.

Why does this happen? There are two basic reasons. First, extremely jealous people don't feel good about themselves. It's likely that they are insecure about life in general, but especially so when it comes to relationships. Maybe they grew up with people telling them how worthless they were or how they didn't measure up to someone else.

Jealous people are dependent on someone else to feel worthwhile, since they don't feel worthwhile on their own. They have to have someone who loves them. Any sign that the other person isn't attentive anymore or is giving attention to someone else makes a jealous person do anything to stop a loved one from leaving. Actually, the opposite usually occurs; jealousy makes the other person want to pull away.

Second, jealous people probably have experienced a personal loss in the past. Some people have powerful fears of being abandoned or of losing love and affection. Maybe a parent, friend, or other loved one died. Or maybe a special relationship ended for other reasons. Breaking up with someone you were in love with can be one such devastating loss.

When a person loses someone, that loss sticks in his or her memory and the person doesn't want to relive it. The person's fear of losing someone else can make jealous feelings explode.

Jealous reactions can also be used in an attempt to control another person. If a loved one gives in to jealous demands – "Don't talk to anyone at the party," "Sit by me the whole time" – the jealous person feels like he or she is in control and has avoided losing the relationship. The problem is that it's only a temporary remedy. Situations like this will happen again. Sooner or later, the loved one will get fed up with jealous demands.

Regardless of why people feel jealous, the result is that they allow jealousy to make them feel bad about relationships that should make them feel good. It doesn't make a lot of sense, but it happens.

The first thing jealous people should realize, and usually don't, is that they do not "own" their friends or anyone else. Friends are not objects. You do not trade them, return them, or throw them away the first time an obstacle gets in the way of your relationship.

A strong relationship is based on faith and confidence, not suspicion and doubt. Real trust is built through countless experiences with another person. You work things out together, sharing good and bad times. You allow your loved one to be a responsible, independent individual. A sense of trust and faith in one another doesn't come easily; you have to work at it.

In the case of Joe and Beth, Beth couldn't stand the thought of someone else sharing part of Joe's life, no matter how small or innocent that part may have been. Jealousy overshadowed trust in a person she really cared for.

That type of jealousy can occur in dating relationships, especially if you have ever experienced the pain of a break-up. You don't want to go through another heartache. But there are limits to what you can expect of other people. Not allowing your date to look at or talk with others is suffocating. Trying to control someone is a sure way to send the relationship down the tubes.

 *The difficulties of life are meant to make us better, not bitter.*

## Overcoming Envy and Jealousy

Is there such a thing as good jealousy? Maybe. If being jealous motivates you to change something in your behavior or to do something posi-tive to make a relationship better, then it can be a positive thing. But remember: Jealousy is a feel-ing. It's how you act on it that determines what will happen in the relationship.

Here are some tips if you're wrestling with jealous feelings:

**1** **Be honest with yourself about how you are feeling.** Remind yourself that you are feeling jealous. There are many ways you can express that feeling. Don't blame another person for what you are feeling.

**2** **When you have your thoughts together, explain your feelings to the person you care about.** Don't hedge on the truth; tell it like it is. Control your emotions but be very honest. If you have a healthy relationship, your friend will understand. Never let people guess why you're acting the way you are. Get problems out in the open and you'll feel better. Directly explaining your jealousy will show the other person how serious you are about trying to make the relation-ship better.

**3** **Turn negative emotions into positive actions.** Instead of doing or saying hurt-ful things, pay more positive attention to your friend. Begin to trust what that person says. It's all right to ask questions about what your friend is doing, but don't become a private investigator. If you're going to have a long-lasting and strong relationship, you have to trust one another.

**4** **There are no guarantees when it comes to relationships.** You may have to take some chances along the way, such as believing and trusting your friend. Please remember that negative feelings can multiply quickly. Stop yourself from dwelling on what's going wrong, and don't let your imagination run wild. Be honest.

You may never feel totally secure in some relationships; that's just the way it is. Maybe you and your friend just aren't the best match. You cannot force someone to love you; all you can do is be a good, caring person and let the chips fall where they may. But one thing is certain: Letting jealousy and envy take control of your behavior will spell disaster for a relationship.

Finding someone who is good and trustworthy may take time; that's why you have to let friendships grow and develop at their own pace. That's also why you should never make a serious commitment before the relationship is strong enough to stand the test of time.

Don't give in to jealousy and envy. Control them. Tell yourself you're going to make all of your relationships better than before. Then do it.

# Prejudice

Prejudice divides people. It is unjust and hurtful. Hate springs quickly from prejudice.

But what is prejudice and why is it so bad? It is a judgment based on fear and ignorance – disliking something or someone we don't know much about. Being prejudiced against people means we form an opinion of them, usually a negative one, without knowing them.

Prejudice has always been around. People have always put other people in categories. Do you think at some point we will wise up?

It's likely that you can think of instances when prejudice was (or is) evident in your life. For example, if a group of kids won't let someone else play with them because he or she is "different," that's prejudice. In your school or neighborhood, do kids hang around only with other kids of their race? Are kids together because they have similar interests or because of skin color? Look around the lunchroom. Is there evidence of prejudice? Do certain groups – athletes, rich kids, smart kids, white kids, African-American kids, Hispanic kids – exclude or pick on others because they don't talk or act like they do? If so, there is prejudicial thinking going on.

## ▶ Ivan's Story

*Ivan is a Native American. He and his family once lived on a reservation, but they moved to a small town off the reservation when he was little. His parents ran a convenience store and gas station and made a fairly good living. Ivan was a good athlete – fast, agile, and very muscular. Even so, Ivan had few friends. Kids in school called him "Tonto," after the Lone Ranger's sidekick. He would be greeted with "How!" or kids would let out a war whoop that sounded like something you'd hear in an old western movie.*

*Ivan kept to himself quite a bit. His shyness made it difficult for him to ask girls out for dates. But he finally got up the nerve to ask Lisa, one of the girls in his math class, to a dance after a Friday night football game. He played well in the game; he recovered a fumble and made nine tackles. It was his best game so far, and he was in a great mood.*

After the game, he met Lisa at the school gym.
They talked a lot and danced a little. They sat at
a table by themselves, barely paying attention to
what everyone else was doing. Every now and
then, they saw other kids looking in their direction and whispering, but they didn't think much
about it. Ivan was telling Lisa about some of the
rituals and beliefs of his tribe, and she thought it
was fascinating. After the dance, Ivan walked Lisa
home. He felt good; he'd finally found a friend.
He was happy and confident for the first time in a
long time.

The next day, his parents found their store
smeared with red spray paint. There were all
kinds of nasty things sprayed on windows and
the driveway. Not only was the store trashed, but
Lisa's house was, too. In her front yard, toilet
paper streamed from trees and hand-painted signs
that said "Squaw" and "Indian Lover" were
stuck in the ground.

Lisa's dad was outraged. But he wasn't mad
at the kids who had vandalized his property. He
was angry with Lisa for crossing racial lines and
dating a Native American. He said she'd shamed
the family, and told her never to talk to Ivan
again. "Don't give him the time of day," he said.

The next Monday at school, the other kids were
cold and distant to Ivan. The girls acted like they
were afraid of him. Most of the guys razzed him or

*laughed at him. After practice that same day, several of the African-American athletes pulled him aside and one said, "Hey, shake it off, man. If one of us had danced with Lisa, her old man would've thrown us in jail for rape. He's the biggest bigot in town and he's got rich friends. He can do what he wants." To make matters worse, Lisa avoided him like he had a contagious disease. Ivan felt lonelier now than ever before. He didn't understand what he had done that was so wrong.*

*Two months later, Ivan returned to the reservation to live with his aunt and uncle. He couldn't live in a town that wouldn't give him a chance, a place that belittled his culture, a place that didn't seem to care about him. He eventually quit school. He couldn't see any future for himself in "white" society. He vowed to stay with his "own people."*

Think about it. What if someone had an opinion of you that you couldn't change, no matter what you did? And what if that opinion was based on nothing more than how you looked or where you lived? Wouldn't you feel hopeless, hurt, and angry? Sure you would.

There is a lot of prejudice in our world. It's not just between countries; it's right there in your own school. The kids in your school are just like kids all over. They categorize and label certain individuals. Kids are singled out because of the way they dress or because of the things they like to do. They are picked on, made fun of, heckled, avoided, or hated.

This has gone on for years; it's not something new. The names change all the time, of course. You know what the kids in your school are called if they don't fit the norm. Someone in your school probably pigeonholes you in a certain group, too, whether you fit into that group or not.

There's prejudice between schools, too. This isn't like a healthy athletic rivalry; this is an unhealthy belief that all kids from a certain school are "the enemy" just because they go to that school. This can lead to territoriality: fights, vandalism, and other acts of violence. Prejudice leads to ugly thinking and ugly deeds.

 *Some people will never escape the prison walls of their own prejudice.*

It's puzzling. Our world is coming together in so many ways – working together, thinking together, sharing new ideas and technology – yet prejudice is still going strong. Sometimes it's like taking one step ahead and two steps back. Why does prejudice thrive? What makes people hold on to untrue thoughts and feelings about others?

First and foremost, prejudice is learned. Babies aren't born with prejudice; children pick it up from their parents, their neighborhood, their friends, and from society in general. Like sponges, they soak up the attitudes of others around them.

Listen to some stand-up comics or watch TV sitcoms. What do you hear? Many times, it's just an endless stream of put-downs and insults. There's a lot of anger and poisonous thinking being shouted at you. The "laugh track" tries to convince you that it's funny stuff, but it's not so funny if you're in the group that's being attacked. Just try telling someone who's the victim of such jokes that it's funny. Prejudice is alive and well.

You know what makes prejudice so widespread? There are many reasons, of course, but one of the simplest is that it makes people feel superior to others. They believe they are better than someone else. They look down on people of other races, religions, backgrounds, and beliefs. On a small scale, there probably are kids in your school who wear the hottest designer fashions and shun kids who wear clothes from the discount store. Those clothes just aren't good enough for someone who's really "in." On a larger scale, there probably are kids who foster hatred for people of another race.

Prejudice allows people to blame other people for the bad in the world. By dividing everything into two categories – good or bad, right or wrong, treasure or trash – prejudiced people can easily say that problems are someone else's fault, not theirs.

**❗** *Prejudice is the child of ignorance.*

People learn to fear different ideas, cultures, rituals, religions, and skin colors. People feel safe when they are around familiar things. When they're faced with someone or something that is different from what they're used to, they become negative, fearful, or hateful. Haven't you felt something like this when you were in an unfamiliar situation?

Please remember that different doesn't mean better or worse; it just means different. And many times it's not the differences between people that cause problems; it is the indifference.

Prejudice determines how people think about and treat other people or groups of people. Their reactions can range from mild to severe, from dislike to hate, or from saying horrible things to doing horrible things.

Let's take a look at some of the categories of prejudice:

**Money or financial status** – the rich looking at poorer people as inferior, the poor looking at richer people as snobs.

**Race** – saying or doing negative things because a person is of another race, nationality, or culture.

**Religion** – believing that your way of worshipping God is the only way, and no other religions should be recognized.

**Disabilities** – avoiding or discriminating against someone with a physical or mental challenge.

**Gender** – believing that the sexes do not have equal rights; labeling activities as either "woman's work" or "man's work."

**Age** – discriminating against the elderly, calling them names and believing they are no longer useful because they are old. Or discriminating against teenagers, believing they're all trouble-makers.

**Occupation** – classifying people by where they work and judging their worth, intelligence, and status by their jobs.

**Appearance** – determining whether a person is good or bad, "with it" or "out of it," by the way he or she looks or dresses.

You see, just about anyone can be prejudiced against someone for something. It's so easy; that's what makes prejudice so widespread. You don't have to think or try to discover the truth, you just have to believe what people tell you. What can be simpler than that?

Take some time to judge yourself before you judge others. Do you treat other people the way you would like to be treated?

 *If someone were to pay you a dime for every kind word you have said about other people, and take back a nickel for every unkind word, would you be rich or poor?*

## Racism

Racists are probably the most prejudiced people of all. They base their opinions of others solely on race. They live in a world of stereotypes. To a racist, everyone in a particular racial group is the same – all lazy or all hard-working, all smart or all dumb, all criminals or all saints, all friends or all enemies. Many racists deny people jobs solely because of the color of their skin. Racism has even started wars.

You probably have racism where you live. It could be blatant or subtle, but it exists. Racists say and do hurtful things to people of a race they consider inferior. Some have gone so far as to injure or kill members of another race. Racism is the worst kind of ignorance.

> ❗ *Wherever there is a human being, there is a chance for kindness.*

## Gangs

Gang members practice prejudice every day. They learn that other people, especially members of other gangs, are the enemy. Gang members are drawn together by a bond: The gang gives them a sense of belonging. There is security in knowing they have other gang members to rely on. Gang members are told what to think, whom to hate, and what to do to other people. Gang members use "colors" and hand signs to identify themselves. They are advertising their beliefs, loyalty, and prejudice.

The way one gang thinks about another is hard to change. They are too busy with acts of violence and hatred to see the goodness in the other side.

## How Not to Be Prejudiced

There are no quick fixes for ridding the world of prejudice. But we have to start somewhere. The starting point is within each of us.

The following ideas can help you overcome your prejudices; then maybe you can help others:

**1** **Take time to become aware of your own prejudices.** Be honest with yourself. Are you going along with the crowd when it comes to judging the goodness in other people or are you trying to get to the truth? Tune in to your attitudes toward others. If your actions say one thing but your conscience tells you something else, try hard to change. Be more kind and respectful.

**2** **Don't "judge a book by its cover."** Do your best to get to know many people. Limiting your friends to a certain "type" of person also limits your personal growth. Nourish your ability to have an open mind. Look at individuals in terms of their friendliness and goodness instead of what they look like or how much they have. You'll end up with better friends.

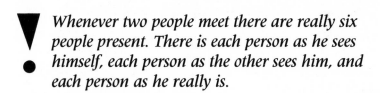

*Whenever two people meet there are really six people present. There is each person as he sees himself, each person as the other sees him, and each person as he really is.*

**3** **Learn more about other cultures.** Don't be afraid to meet and talk with kids from different races, religions, and ethnic groups. Put yourself in their position to see how they view the world. You will gain a new awareness of why others believe what they believe. This is true empathy – respecting the feelings of others and what they are going through in their lives. Look at situations through their eyes, and you'll be surprised.

Read about different cultures. Learn about their histories. Go to ethnic fairs. Try to understand how various traditions came about. Remember: Prejudice is strengthened by ignorance; it is weakened by knowledge.

**4** **Avoid calling other people names.** Put-downs, racial slurs, hurtful jokes, and other forms of name-calling lead to bad feelings and retaliation. There are hundreds of nasty, disrespectful names that people have for one another. They keep stereotypes alive.

Think how you would feel if people verbally attacked you, your family, or your heritage. If people do say prejudiced things about you, don't make malicious comments in return. Be tolerant of their ignorance, and try to forgive them.

**5** **Set a good example.** Try to treat other people with the respect and dignity every human being deserves. For example, take time to get to know an elderly person. Perhaps you could ask at a nursing home for the name of a resident who has no family nearby. You could visit regularly, read to him or her, or run errands. There are many ways you can help others overcome prejudice by sharing your gifts of friendship and caring. Your reward will be a good feeling because helping someone in need is the right thing to do.

Finally, you have to truly believe that people are more similar than different. We all are human beings, sometimes weak, sometimes strong. We all have hopes and dreams, frustrations and fears. We all want good families and successful lives. We all want to love and be loved. When you look at other people, don't think of superficial differences like skin color or money; think instead of our common humanity and goodness.

 *A great deal of what we see depends on what we are looking for.*

# Anger and Agression

Anger is a common human emotion. Sometimes getting angry is healthy. It can motivate us to change ourselves. Unfortunately, many people don't handle their anger constructively. It is a harmful force in their lives.

## Shawn's Story

*All of the guys Shawn hung around with called him "Psycho." They didn't know when he would blow up next. Shawn did bizarre things when he was angry. Anything reachable was in danger of being thrown, broken, kicked, or hit, including humans.*

*The guys remember one time when Shawn was really scary. His family had just bought a puppy, a pudgy little German shepherd mixed-breed with floppy ears and beautiful tan and charcoal markings around its face and eyes. Shawn was having a party before the NFL Game of the Week. He was trying to get the puppy to attack a toy doll. The puppy would roll around and play with it for a little while, then become curious about something else and waddle off to make new discoveries. This angered Shawn. He wanted a dog that would obey him and make other people afraid. He wanted an attack dog, not some wimpy little mutt. This pup wasn't mean at all.*

*Shawn picked up the dog and began slapping and shaking it. The puppy was frightened; it squealed and whimpered and tried to wrest itself from Shawn's huge hands. Shawn squeezed it tighter and yelled, "I'm the boss! I'm the boss!" The puppy continued its painful squealing and wriggling. The rest of the kids were stunned. One of the girls told Shawn to "cool it" and leave the puppy alone. Shawn yelled and swore at her and told her to get out of his house.*

*Shawn was really out of control now. He threw the puppy across the room. It hit the hardwood floor and careened into the living room wall. As it struggled to get up, Shawn grabbed it again, threw it into his bedroom, and slammed the door.*

*That dog is now so mean that none of the guys want to go to Shawn's house unless it's outside.*

*Shawn had appeared twice in juvenile court on assault charges. Both times, the charges were dropped. Basically, the judge lectured him, told him to control his temper, and threatened to lock him up if he ever did it again. But no action was ever taken against him. Shawn's dad was a police officer and the judge told him to keep a closer eye on his son. Whenever Shawn got into trouble, his dad beat the daylights out of him. That didn't make much difference, though; Shawn was used to the beatings. He figured it would just make him more of a man.*

*One day at school, the English teacher was asking questions about American poets. English certainly didn't rank very high on Shawn's list of interests. In fact, he thought the whole class was lousy. He didn't know why he had to take any class that studied what a bunch of sissies wrote. Shawn was daydreaming when the teacher called on him to identify the poet who wrote, "Stopping by Woods on a Snowy Evening." Shawn didn't have the slightest idea. He closed his eyes and tried to think of the name of any American poet so he could at least give an answer. All of the other kids were looking at him, waiting for his response. Finally, Shawn blurted out, "William Shakespeare!" The class laughed. It struck the class brain as particularly hysterical and he said to Shawn, "Shakespeare wasn't even an American!" As the kid laughed, Shawn glared at him and told him to shut his mouth and mind his own business.*

*Shawn fumed for the rest of the class period. How dare a bunch of geeks laugh at him. The more he thought about it, the madder he got. He thought he was going to explode. When the bell rang, he flew out of his seat, bumped his chest into the chest of the smart kid, stared him in the eyes, and said, "You're dead meat." The teacher over-heard Shawn and told him to go to the principal's office for threatening another student. Shawn just stood there glaring at her before mumbling, "Whatever."*

*He was really steamed now. He began walking down the hall, then told himself, "The hell with this!" He made a quick about-face and headed back. He caught up with the kid he had threat-ened and slammed him against a row of lockers. Shawn was screaming obscenities now. The more he yelled, the madder he got. He started beating the kid, punching him in the face, stomach, and ribs. Kids bolted out of their classrooms, but no one was brave enough to do anything to stop his onslaught. It took three teachers to pull Shawn off the other kid. Angry tears spewed from Shawn's eyes, as though they had been there for years, screaming to be released.*

*Shawn was sent to a detention facility for vio-lent teenagers. The other kid was hospitalized with a broken jaw and cracked ribs. The other kid's parents are suing Shawn's parents for the physical and emotional attack on their son.*

Shawn is like many people who can't handle anger appropriately. Their anger is terribly destructive. And just as in Shawn's case, when people don't know how to control their anger, someone usually gets hurt.

Many kids learn that anger is a way of life. They've seen their father or mother, brother or sister, close friend, or other role model get angry and lash out at others. They have been taught that anger is a way to get what they want. In other words, they have been taught that showing anger and being aggressive is okay.

The problem is, anger is not okay, and it rarely solves problems. In fact, anger that is not channeled in some constructive way causes more problems than it ever solves.

It's important to realize that there is a difference between anger and aggression. Anger is a feeling. Aggression is a behavior. The same distinctions exist between other feelings and behaviors as well. For example, sadness is a feeling, but crying is a behavior – a way to show your sadness. Just as you can be sad without crying, you can be angry without being aggressive. That's an important difference.

There's also a distinction between "just anger" – that which is morally justifiable – and "unjust anger" – that which is not justifiable. For example, if someone steals something of yours, you have a right to be angry. It's justified. But being angry for no apparent reason or being angry all the time is wrong. Some people seem to be mad at the world. If someone looks at them wrong, they feel they have a right to "go off." That's an example of unjust anger.

It's also important to know that there are two kinds of aggression – verbal and physical. Verbal aggression takes the form of threats, put-downs, or insults. People use verbal aggression to "attack" other people with harsh words. Physical aggression, of course, is attacking by slapping, pushing, hitting, and kicking. Both types of aggression hurt other people.

Some people think that there is something wrong with them if they get angry. They are mistaken. There's nothing wrong with getting angry. What matters is how people express their anger. Please remember that. When anger is expressed as aggression, there is a problem.

## What Can You Do?

There are three basic ways you can deal with your anger: hold it inside, take it out on someone or something else, or release it constructively.

Holding it inside means that you won't hurt anyone or anything else, so that's good. However, holding it inside can be unhealthy. Many people who do this end up with heartburn, headaches, and ulcers. Angry feelings are stuffed inside for so long that they finally have to burst out. When you release pent-up anger in a sudden emotional explosion, you are likely to say or do something that you will regret later. You will end up in trouble.

 *When I hide my emotions, my stomach keeps score.*

Taking your anger out on someone else is not a good option. It only makes the other person angry, too; then he or she wants to get back at you. Depending on how severe your behavior is, arguments or fights can start. People can get hurt. Regardless of what happens, it's fairly certain that neither person is going to feel good about the other. People who take out their anger on someone else are frequently blaming the other person for making them angry, as if they had an "On/Off" anger switch that the other person controlled. That's not true. Only you can give someone permission to make you angry. Sure, other people can do irritating things. But you are, or should be, the one in control of how you react.

Many adult relationships fail because one person unloads angry, pent-up feelings on the other. When they finally burst out, the person's anger overcomes everything else and damaging things are said or done. Relationships suffer tremendously when that happens.

On the other hand, there are times when taking anger out on an object is okay. There are many anger control gimmicks on the market – rubber dolls to squeeze, punching bags to hit, worry stones that let you rub your troubles away – that can help reduce some anger or tension. You also can hit or yell into a pillow, or do something else to release a little steam – if the situation is appropriate.

But there are times when you just can't do these things. If you're angry at a police officer who gives you a speeding ticket, you can't kick the side of the squad car to release your anger. That is aggressive – not to mention illegal- behavior, and it will be dealt with aggressively in return. Similarly, if you're mad while you're driving a car, you can't smash into someone to release your anger. You could hurt someone, wreck your car, and set yourself up for a huge lawsuit. So, although taking your anger out on something is sometimes an option, it's not always possible.

▼ *There is no more terrible sight than anger*
**!** *in action.*

The best choice is to learn how to deal constructively with your anger. Find a way to cool down before you do something hurtful or get into trouble. The following tips might help:

**1** **Recognize when you're starting to get angry.** Most people know when they cross the line from being calm to being angry. But what happens in between? Most people don't pay attention to the signals their minds and bodies give them.

Be aware of what you are doing and thinking. When your mind first begins to cloud up with angry thoughts, tell yourself, "Stop it! Calm down. Put on the brakes." Don't react on impulse. People who suddenly lash out at the nearest person or thing are in for trouble.

When people start to get angry, a series of physical reactions usually kicks into gear – the heart pounds, the face gets flushed, muscles tense up, the face or hands get sweaty. Pay attention to what your body is doing. Recognize your anger warning signs early so that you can control them.

There also are different levels of anger, ranging from being annoyed to being furious. Learn to recognize what anger level you usually reach. Squelch the urge to explode.

Admitting you're angry is okay. It's only bad when you show anger in harmful, destructive

71

ways. When you feel yourself starting to "lose it," have a positive plan for dealing with your anger. Stop it before it gets out of control. You can do it.

**!** *Anger is one letter away from danger.*

**2 Figure out what makes you angry.** Take some time when you're calm to think about the things that make you angry. Is it one person who says or does things that bug you? Do you get upset at a certain group of people? Do you get upset only in certain situations or at certain times during the day? Do you get mad at yourself when you make a mistake and then let it ruin your whole day?

Think back to the last several times you were steaming mad. What caused your anger? You have to be very honest with yourself and not blame others for what happens to you. Taking responsibility for your actions is extremely difficult. Look at your behavior and see what you can change, then make an anger-control plan. You will find that situations aren't nearly as tough to deal with when you can control yourself.

**3 Practice positive "self-talk."** Catch yourself when you're starting to get mad. Don't let angry thoughts fly around your brain, colliding with one another. Recognize your anger warning signals and realize that you can control it. Positive self-talk is one way.

Positive self-talk helps you stop negative thoughts and quickly slam them into reverse. Think healthy, constructive thoughts in order to control your anger. That may sound kind of dumb when you feel like you're ready to explode, but you can do it. Tell yourself, "I'm really upset right now. I need to calm down," or "I'm getting angry right now, but I'm in control." Repeat these phrases over and over to get your mind off reacting aggressively.

 *Attitudes are often more important than intelligence.*

It's very important to remember not to dwell on your anger. Don't let angry thoughts and feelings run wild. That's like pouring gasoline on a fire. Say positive things to yourself instead, things that indicate you're in control of your feelings. If you let anger control what you do, your life will be one crisis after another. Tell yourself, "I am in charge of my own life."

**4** **Find a healthy way to release your anger.** After the immediate situation has passed, take some time to release any leftover tension or negative emotions by doing something that relaxes you. Physical exercise is a healthy habit to develop. If you are in a situation in which you are likely to get angry, use self-talk and tell yourself, "I'm going to keep my cool now. Later I'm going to work out. That will make me feel better." Running, doing push-ups or sit-ups, walking, swimming, riding a bike – these are all good ways to deal with stress and tension. Many people relax by hitting golf balls, kicking a football or soccer ball, or hitting baseballs or softballs. Exercise has a great effect on the human body. It releases chemicals that help you cope with tough times. If you don't exercise regularly now, start right away. You'll notice a difference.

Other people deal with stress and tension by relaxing in less physical ways – reading, working or playing games on the computer, doing crossword puzzles, or watching TV.

There are lots of other ways to calm yourself. Maybe you can count to 10 or wear a rubber band around your wrist and snap it when you feel yourself becoming upset. You can get a good luck charm and rub it in your hand when you're mad. These are positive ways to help you keep your temper. Find one that works for you.

You will find that it feels great to have self-control. Pat yourself on the back and feel good about dealing constructively with your anger.

**❗** *You can't shake hands with a clenched fist.*

**5** **Learn how to talk about your anger with others, especially thoughtful and caring adults and friends.** Parents, teachers, counselors, and other trusted adults can help by telling you how they've learned to control their anger. They get angry too, and they know very well the negative things that can happen when anger is expressed in inappropriate ways.

Talk to a friend about your anger, and about how you want to change. Many times, just being able to tell someone you're angry makes you feel better. You also can join an anger-control group if you feel you need the help of others with the same problem.

**6** **Learn to relax your body and your mind.** Find a healthy way to relax. Some people visualize – that means they think of images, like the anger draining from their bodies. They might see their anger flowing like lava oozing out of a volcano or flying softly away like pigeons being released from a cage. Or they may imagine a quiet scene where they are comfortable and relaxed.

Some people practice deep breathing. It helps them calm down and it may work for you, too. Learn to relax your facial muscles by opening your mouth as if you were yawning. Stretch your arms over your head as you take a deep breath and then slowly lower your arms as you exhale.

These techniques work for a lot of people. If you think they might help you and you want more information, there are many books on relaxation you can read.

**7** **Be aware of your feelings.** People have many feelings besides anger. However, anger is so powerful that others sometimes go unrecognized. For example, you could be feeling sad, hurt, jealous, afraid, disliked, left out, or frustrated. You can have a combination of different feelings at the same time. However, your behavior may indicate that you are angry. Once you learn to recognize what you're feeling, you can find a way to deal with it or at least explain it to others.

Being aware of feelings and talking about them can reduce your stress level so you can resolve the situation. For example, you might say, "I'm feeling depressed right now. I need to listen to some music to help me feel better," or "I'm frustrated because of my English grade. I need to learn how to ask for help."

You can learn to deal with anger in a positive way. Like all of the other skills described in this book, it will take practice. Notice small improvements and praise yourself for them. Gradually, you will learn how to deal with your anger and prevent it from getting the best of you.

## When Anger Leads to Aggression and Violence

Everyone needs to understand that it is wrong to hurt other people. Much of what is wrong in our world stems from the beast called anger. If anger is causing you or someone you know to do aggressive and hurtful things to others, the following suggestions may help.

**1** **Look at the consequences of your actions.** Look at how unhappy you are and how unhappy you make others by being aggressive. Does everyone seem to be against you? Are you losing friends and getting into trouble because of your anger? See the pain that anger and aggression cause in your life.

**2** **Learn the value of being gentle.** Aggressive people often have been the victims of aggression. That's how they learn that aggressive behaviors can control others. Remember that it hurts. Put yourself in the victim's place. Sit down and talk to an adult and describe how you think it feels to be a victim of your anger, hostility, and threats. This is how you learn the value of being gentler.

**3** **Realize that it is wrong, both morally and legally, to hit, hurt, or intimidate someone.** Look in the newspaper and see what fines and court sentences are given to people who have hurt others. Real-life consequences are eye-openers. You have to have the courage to admit you were wrong. You have to "lay it all on the table" and be honest with yourself and your friends. Only then can you begin to rebuild your life in constructive ways.

Most important, find ways to make up for the bad things you have done to others. Apologize, if appropriate. Pay for anything that you've damaged. Do something that puts you back on the right track. You can't undo what has happened but you can do something to correct your wrongs.

**4** **Practice being generous and helpful.** Research shows that the happiest teenagers are those who are generous and helpful with family and friends, get along with teachers and other adults, tell the truth, and volunteer to help others. Being nice is not a sign of weakness; it shows strength. It helps you as well as others.

**5** **Learn to talk to someone about negative feelings.** Humans have a capacity to listen and understand when they are called on to help. Many will help if you give them a chance. It is unhealthy to keep things bottled up inside you. Learn to share your feelings with others that you can trust.

**6** **Develop your capacity for compassion.** You say that you have suffered a lot in your life, right? If you have suffered, then you have the capacity for compassion. You can learn to feel sympathy for the person you are hurting by your aggression.

**7** **Help others who have a similar problem.** You can be a role model for other aggressive people. When you improve your own skills and become a nicer person, other people will like you more. Being generous, honest, and helpful doesn't mean you're corny or wimpy. These are positive and courageous qualities. You'll gain the respect and admiration of other people, and you'll feel better about yourself.

**!** *The amount of pain we inflict upon others is directly proportional to the amount we feel within ourselves.*

# Teasing

Has anyone ever made fun of you or something you've done? Have you ever been ridiculed in front of others? It stings like crazy, doesn't it? It probably made you mad or self-conscious. You may have wanted to cry. Other people can be cruel and what they say about us can cut like a knife.

Teasing and bullying (more on bullying later) are aggressive and hurtful behaviors. Both teasing and bullying can be torture to people who are the victims.

## Lisa's Story

*Lisa was overweight. She had always been the biggest one in her class, even in grade school. Her parents told her that she was just "big-boned," but that explanation didn't provide much consolation. Lisa wasn't athletic or coordinated, and she hated going to gym class. She felt like an outsider most of the time.*

*Lisa wasn't very attractive and boys rarely paid attention to her – except when they needed a target. Of all the students in her school, she got singled out the most as the butt of cruel jokes and name-calling. It became a sadistic game to everyone – seeing who could say the rudest and crudest things about Lisa. And they called her those names to her face.*

*These taunts upset Lisa terribly. It's no wonder she didn't feel good about herself. And it's easy to understand why going to school each day was a living hell for her. She didn't understand why everyone was so cruel to her; she had never done anything bad to them.*

*When kids made fun of her, tears would well up in her eyes and she would shake her head as if she could make the words go away. She would clutch her books tightly to her chest and try to get away as quickly as possible. Several times she had her eyes closed to keep in the tears and bumped into something. This only served as more ammunition for the other kids.*

*Sometimes guys would make kissing sounds and pucker up their lips. They would say sexual things to her, and then everyone would laugh like crazy. She thought they were all sick and disgust-*

*ing and wished they would just disappear. It hurt her badly.*

*Lisa often cried herself to sleep at night, thinking about what the kids had said. She remembered their sadistic faces and heard their sarcastic laughing and taunting. And she frequently woke up with red, puffy eyes, a trait that certainly didn't go unnoticed by her classmates the next day.*

*In geography class one Monday, the teacher was talking about the damage a recent earthquake had done in Peru. He showed pictures of smashed houses, crushed cars, and tons of rubble. One of the kids shouted out, "Hey, I know why. Lisa was just there on vacation! And she flew on a jumbo jet! Alone!" The class thought that was hysterically funny. Their laughter was still thundering in her ears as she ran out of the classroom and went home.*

*Lisa finished high school by taking a correspondence course at home. She didn't ever want to be around those kids again.*

## Why Do People Tease Others?

There are two things that seem to make teasing fun. First, some people like to "push someone's buttons." They find cruel enjoyment in saying and doing things that irritate, upset, or hurt other people. There's some kind of satisfaction in watching another person squirm or lose control. The more a person reacts, the more the teasing continues.

Second, whoever is doing the teasing gets an "audience reaction." Other kids laugh at the antics, and the teaser gets a form of peer approval and acceptance. It's a way to get a reputation within a group.

 *Words are like arrows. Once they're let loose, they do not return.*

Remember the old saying, "Sticks and stones can break my bones, but words can never hurt me"? But words do hurt when they are purposely used to make someone feel bad.

Teasing is only fun for the one doing the teasing. For the victim, teasing can hurt terribly, especially when it "strikes a nerve" – when the teasing zeroes in on something you are sensitive about. It's like the whole world is pointing a finger at you, laughing and mocking your shortcomings. You feel as if all of your flaws are being examined under a magnifying glass. When other kids see your embarrassment or discomfort, you become an obvious target for more teasing.

People who tease sometimes try to soften the blow. They may say, "I was just kidding," or "I didn't mean anything by it," or "What's the matter? Can't you take a joke?" Don't you hate that? You know it's an excuse and a cop-out. The teasing words can't be taken back. In some cases, the teasing really may have started out as a joke, but if it hurts, it's no joke. If you've ever been a victim, you know how painful it can be.

Is there ever a time when teasing is okay? Maybe. Teasing between friends can be fun if each person knows that it's not done out of meanness or disrespect. Teasing can be a sparring match of words between you and your friends. You can have a few laughs and no one gets upset. Good friends should know how to "take it" as well as how to "dish it out." But not everyone has a relationship like that, and no one should be expected to put up with cruel teasing. Teasing kids you don't know very well goes beyond the boundaries of harmless fun.

Teasing can take various forms: calling names, gossiping, making jokes that exaggerate a part of a person's body or personality, laughing or pointing at another person, making faces, or whistling. Teasing can be direct, such as a face-to-face insult or put-down, or it can be much subtler. But when someone is singled out and made fun of, it's wrong.

The victim is usually someone who doesn't fit the "norm" for the group – someone who is bigger or smaller, less popular, weaker, less attractive, physically or mentally disabled, or who is of a different race or religion. The victim could be someone another person envies.

Sometimes a person can make changes to stop the teasing. For example, if someone is made fun of for poor hygiene, he or she can learn to shower every day and wear clean clothes. At other times, the things people are teased about can't be altered. You cannot change your race or a physical disability, for example.

Regardless of who the victim is or what the reason for the teasing is, when a person belittles another person, it's wrong. It's cruel and childish.

## How to Respond to Teasing

There are several ways to respond to teasing; you'll have to find a way that fits your personality and situation. First, you have to have a serious talk with yourself. Convince yourself that you can keep your cool, no matter what someone says to you. Tell yourself that teasing is not going to get the best of you. You can develop a "tough skin" that makes the words bounce off you and fall harmlessly aside.

Given the notion that teasing continues because it gets you upset, your first goal should be to take the sting out of the comments. Don't give the teaser the satisfaction of seeing you react. This isn't easy, but it often works. If the teaser doesn't get the desired reaction – meaning if you don't get upset or mad – it's likely that the fun of teasing will be taken away. Think of it this way: If there's no air inflating a hot air balloon, it isn't going to fly. The same is true when you don't allow the teasers to get a rise out of you.

**❗** *One thing about silence – it can't be repeated.*

Find a way that doesn't feed into what the teasing is all about. If the teasing isn't too personal or doesn't last too long, maybe you can just ignore it. Smile and "play it off." You could say, "I don't like it when you put me down," and then just walk away. You could respond with humor by saying, "Thanks, I needed that." For example, if someone calls you "stupid." You can say, "No kidding. I don't have the brains God gave a crowbar." Sometimes a quick comeback can work.

If you can develop the art of handling the teasing without appearing upset, it takes a lot of the fun away from the teaser. You may have to try a different plan for different people. You will have to be patient; the teasing isn't going to stop right away. And it's absolutely vital that you stay calm so that your response will work. It's a good idea to practice what you're going to say or do if someone teases you again.

You also have to convince yourself that, regardless of what the teaser says, you're a better person than he is. You don't have to lower yourself to that level. Don't tease the person in return. That's just asking for things to get worse. Feel good about yourself and the fact that you're sensitive and mature enough not to make fun of others' shortcomings. Any person who takes pleasure in teasing others is bound to make a lot of enemies. People can't step on other people's feelings for long and expect to be well-liked. Take some comfort in knowing that you're too good a person to sink to the teaser's level.

 *Big people talk about ideas; little people talk about other people.*

Even if you find a way to stop or reduce the teasing, it's quite likely that the words that were said will continue to bother you. If that happens, talk to someone you can trust. Talk to your close friends. If the teasing verges on cruelty and harassment, talk to a teacher, counselor, or your parents. Ask them for advice. Maybe there is a way to change whatever it is you always get teased about. Maybe there is an option that you haven't tried. If you feel bad about the teasing, remember that the people close to you can help ease the hurt. At times like those, it's nice to have comfort and support from people who care.

# Bullies

Everyone knows a bully. They lurk around every school and playground in the nation. And for every bully, there has to be at least one victim. Every school has kids who have been pushed around or picked on. If you're a victim, you know it's a humiliating and frightening experience.

## Derek's Story

*Derek is shy and doesn't have any close friends. When he was little, he was sick a lot with respiratory illnesses. He missed school fairly often because of his chronic asthma. Since he was five years old, he's had to carry a pocket inhaler. His breathing problems kept him from participating in sports and gym class.*

*During his sophomore year, Derek volunteered to be the basketball team's student manager. This pleased his parents because he had never joined any activities or clubs before, and they encour-*

*aged Derek to stick with it. In fact, they told him that if he lasted the whole season, they would buy him the computer he wanted. Derek really looked forward to getting the computer and was excited about being the student manager.*

*Most of the guys on the team treated Derek okay, but there was one boy, Aaron, who loved to pick on him. Aaron frequently taunted Derek by calling him names. Not once did Aaron call Derek by his real name. Aaron often made menacing faces or spat at Derek when no one was looking. Sometimes Aaron stuck his tongue out and then slid his index finger in a slicing motion across his throat. Aaron's attacks on Derek got worse. He cursed at Derek, threatened to "jack his jaw," twirled up towels and snapped him, "accidentally" bumped into him, pushed him against walls, and tripped him when he walked by. Several team members told Aaron to knock if off and quit picking on Derek, but they never stepped in to stop anything Aaron did. Aaron was tough and he was big, and they really didn't like Derek that much anyway – at least not well enough to risk getting hurt.*

*Derek handled most of the name-calling okay, but physical harassment scared him. He would start shaking and close his eyes, or plead with Aaron to stop. One time Derek cried and that disgusted Aaron, because he hated weakness.*

*One day Derek was picking up towels and uniforms in the locker room when Aaron walked in. The other guys were gone. Aaron had forgotten his gym bag and came back to get it. He saw Derek and said, "Well, what do we have here? Little runt doing the big boys' laundry?" Derek didn't say anything and continued working. Aaron said, "Hey, boy, I'm talking to you!"*

*Derek's hands were trembling and he meekly said, "Don't hurt me." That was just what Aaron wanted to see and hear. He launched into a tirade about how Derek was a momma's boy, and how he didn't have the guts to put up a fight.*

*Derek wanted to escape but Aaron had the doorway blocked. In desperation, he threw the load of wet towels in Aaron's face and ran out the door. This infuriated Aaron. He caught up with Derek and began choking him. Finally, Aaron let him go. Derek collapsed onto the floor, gasping for air. He was dizzy and couldn't catch his breath. Aaron bent over, pointed his finger at him, and said, "I hope you learned your lesson, punk. And you better not tell anyone about this." Then he punched Derek's arm and ran out.*

*Derek quit his job as student manager. He never told anyone why. His parents were angry with him for giving up, but he didn't tell them what really happened. He just said the job wasn't for him. Derek felt that if he said anything, Aaron would do something worse to him.*

## Profile of a Bully

Bullies want to control other people. They have found that violence works, and that fearful victims will obey if they are pushed around enough. They like to pick on kids who are alone, and they often pick on the same kid over and over.

Bullies may intimidate, threaten, pick fights, push and hit other kids, steal money or possessions from someone, or ruin another person's property. Bullies are thugs. They usually pick on smaller, weaker kids because they're easy marks; they are easy to beat up or push around. Many times, bullies have followers – kids who may or may not be bullies themselves – who tag along for whatever status or reputation being around the bully can bring.

Why does a bully choose these aggressive and harmful behaviors?

**1** **A bully wants control over another person.** This may be because the bully is dissatisfied with his or her own life and wants the power that comes with control.

**2** **A bully doesn't know how to get attention in positive and acceptable ways.** Therefore, the bully uses force. He or she has to make people afraid so they will give in.

**3** **A bully is antisocial.** This means he or she is rude and hostile on purpose. Bullies don't respect the rights of others. They believe that inflicting pain on others is fun. It's a cruel game, to be sure, but being the tough guy becomes a way of life.

**4** **A bully feels justified in picking on others and is probably even proud of it.** Bullies don't necessarily have low self-esteem; on the contrary, they frequently feel pretty good about themselves. In a bully's mind, weaker, smaller, and younger kids deserve to be picked on. The bully also may resent kids who are sensitive, which a bully considers to be wimpy.

**5** **A bully learned how to bully.** This is a very important point. He or she didn't wake up one morning and suddenly begin pushing people around. It's quite possible that the bully comes from a family that uses force, physical punishment, or aggression to settle problems or deal with other people. The bully probably learned as a little kid that throwing temper tantrums and pushing people around helped him or her get things, especially attention. For most kids, even negative attention is better than no attention at all. Yelling, screaming, throwing things, fighting, and always "getting in someone's face" are the things the bully learned as a child.

> ❗ *No person ever becomes very good or very bad suddenly.*

## Profile of a Victim

Victims frequently have a history of being rejected by the rest of the kids. They may be insecure, fearful, oversensitive, or lacking in assertiveness. They may do irritating things: act "hyper," argue and whine, or try to join in when they aren't wanted. Many times, victims are on the "fringe" and have never really fit in. Most victims are physically weaker than their bully counterparts.

Victims have to be easy prey for their attackers. A bully isn't going to be involved in a fair fight. Kids often become victims when they first enter junior high or high school. The older and bigger kids pick on them, and they just aren't big or strong enough to defend themselves.

Victims don't have a lot of "tough" friends to protect them. Some don't have many friends at all, which is one reason they're picked on.

## How to Deal with a Bully

Kids who carry aggressive and antisocial behaviors into adolescence need to change. But change like that isn't easy. Bullying becomes a way of life, and it satisfies a need to control other people. If bullies don't change now, violence and aggression will plague them as adults. Bullies are likely to commit crimes and get in trouble with the law. They may not be able to hold a job because co-workers won't put up with being pushed around. They probably will have difficulty maintaining a caring relationship. Any way you look at it, the future looks bleak for someone who can't, or won't, control aggressive behavior. Violence breeds more violence. In one way, you can feel sorry for a bully, because "what goes around, comes around."

**❗ *Time wounds all heels.***

It's obvious that bullies need to learn how to be helpful and friendly to others, and how to care about others. Unfortunately, the people who know this best – the victims – probably aren't going to be able to bring about this change. A bully has to make the decision and the effort to change. And the bully needs to receive negative consequences for threatening and intimidating other kids.

But victims of bullies can take steps to protect themselves and make living with a bully easier. This involves learning how to be more assertive and confident. That sounds good in theory, of course, but accomplishing it is no small task for someone who has a history of giving in to a bully's demands. So, if you are being victimized, the first thing you must do is reach deep down inside yourself and muster up all of the courage and confidence you can find.

> ❗ *Don't expect to make others as you wish them to be if you can't make yourself as you wish to be.*

Here are some other suggestions on how to deal with a bully and stop being a victim:

**1** **Learn how to make friends.** This sounds like a simple solution, but if you don't have a lot of friends now, it won't be easy. If you do things that people don't like, learn how to change and be likable. You have to develop a sense of humor and increase your confidence about being around others.

No matter what stage of life you are in, problems are always easier to face when you have friends. They can help you. If you have friends to hang out with, it's also less likely that a bully will attack you. There is strength in numbers. The bully may not want to challenge a whole group of kids because he feels outnumbered or thinks they may retaliate. Another important advantage is the emotional support friends give you.

If you've been rejected by other kids in the past, you're really going to have to work at developing good friendship skills. You can't force friendship on someone; your behaviors show others what kind of person you are, and if those behaviors turn people off, you need to change them so people will want to be around you. A good start would be to look for kids who share your interests. Learn how to start a conversation and keep it going. Learn how to give your opinion without turning people off. The first book in this series talks about friendship skills you can develop. Give them a try.

Some of those skills may even help you find a weak spot in the bully's armor. This doesn't mean that your goal is to make the bully your friend; that's pretty far-fetched. Your goal is to do things that make it less likely that you will be picked on.

Practice things you can say to show you are confident. For example, learn how to give compliments. Make them short; don't overdo it. Say "Nice job," or "That's cool," when the person does something good. Even bullies like to hear praise.

Practice several come-back lines. Keep them short, too. Make sure you don't say something sarcastic about the bully. Respond to a problem or what a bully says and use an "I" statement. For example, if someone calls you a wimp, say something like, "Yeah, I'm working on that." Whatever you decide to say, say it with confidence. You may have to try different things to find out what works, but don't give up. There is no magic phrase that will turn the bully into a saint. You're just trying things that will take some of the pressure off you.

If you're told to mind your own business or the bully looks like he's going to do something aggressive, then just leave. And always try to find a neutral time – certainly not when a bully has an audience of "friends" who could gang up on you – to talk to the bully. Practice some very basic friendship skills that will help you peel that "victim" tag off your back.

 *The average enemy doesn't know what to do if you suddenly forgive him.*

Another thing you can do is talk to a trusted adult who can give you some guidance and suggestions. Gather up the courage to say, "Other kids don't like me. Help me find a way to make friends." A teacher, counselor, family member – someone is out there to lend you a helping hand. Grab on and hold tightly and learn how to be liked. It can be done.

Everyone – bully as well as victim – needs help sometimes. A little kindness and understanding can go a long way.

**2** **Avoid the bully.** It stands to reason that you can't be pushed around if you're not around to be pushed. This may sound like the "chicken" way out, but you certainly don't want to get hurt again. Sometimes it's best to avoid or leave situations where it's likely that you or someone else could get hurt. If you're at school, you can possibly stay close to a teacher. Don't set yourself up to be picked on by being in situations where it's obvious that you could get hurt.

On the other hand, avoiding a bully isn't always possible. You can't stop going to school or avoid every place where the bully might show up. And when it is obvious to the bully that you are avoiding him or her, it means the bully is doing exactly what he or she wants – controlling you. Avoidance only works in certain situations.

**3** **Get other kids to help you.** It's important to remember that bullies don't bully everyone, just a select few. Other kids – usually those who are fairly self-confident and assertive – tend to get left alone. There are more of these kids than there are bullies and victims, and a bully might even get along with some of them or at least respect what they say.

It's this large core of students who can help by using peer pressure to try to get the bully to change. They can step in when they see the bully harassing or attacking the victim. Maybe they can talk the bully out of antagonizing other kids. They might even be able to encourage the bully to join a sports team like soccer, softball, volleyball, football, or hockey, where aggressive behavior within set rules and guidelines is rewarded.

Bullies feed on recognition and attention, so if someone he respects or runs around with thinks his behavior is bad, it may help turn him around.

Similarly, this peer group should be more willing to help the victim and be more understanding of how it must feel to be picked on. This group needs to let victims know why other kids don't like them. If victims are given a chance to change, maybe they will be more likable.

Both victims and bullies need to receive praise and positive attention when they learn how to get along with others. There are kids in school systems who have done a wonderful job of helping solve problems just like this.

**4** **Stop acting like a victim.** This is very important. Weakness attracts bullies like flies to a picnic. Stand up straight, and don't fidget. Look people in the eye instead of looking down at the ground. Speak with a firm voice instead of mumbling. These behaviors show confidence and make it less likely that you will be picked on.

Bullies like to get a reaction. If you cry, whine, respond angrily, or run away, you just give the bully more fuel for the fire. The pain and torment you express through your behavior is like a reward for the bully. Therefore, you need to remove the reward. Don't give the bully the satisfaction of seeing you upset.

Don't get this confused with confronting the bully face-to-face. You're not going to fight or retaliate. This isn't a Hollywood movie where a scrawny kid suddenly learns karate and then kicks the daylights out of the bad guy. It's good stuff for a script, but it rarely happens in real life. What you are going to do is change the way you behave – appearing confident instead of fearful – so you can stop being an obvious target.

**5** **If you are being bullied or harassed frequently or cruelly, you need to talk to someone about the problem.** Some kids who are bullied are afraid or embarrassed to talk about the problem. Some don't want to "tattle" because they think it will cause other kids to dislike them even more. Others are worried that the bully will find out and increase the attacks.

But if you are being tormented by a bully, you have to tell someone you trust and respect – your parents, your friends, a teacher or counselor, or some other trusted adult. If you're afraid of being hurt, it is a serious matter. It's not tattling. It's reporting violent behavior that needs to stop.

**6** **Make your school aware of the problem.** Bullying occurs often in schools because a large group of kids are together. It's easy for bullies to find victims. They can spot weakness immediately and will pounce on any opportunity to find a target.

School personnel should be aware of and respond to bullying behaviors in your school. No school should let harassment and abuse continue. The bully's parents should be notified about their child's hostility toward others. Kids can't, and shouldn't, be completely responsible for changing the bully's behavior. A bully needs serious negative consequences if he or she is to change, and not being accepted or liked by other kids often isn't enough. Adults may have to step in and provide effective consequences, or at least create a safe environment for all kids.

Some bullies have severe emotional problems and need professional help. They may even wind up in jail. But some of them really do want to change and can change. Bullies need to learn socially acceptable ways to gain approval. And victims need to stand up for themselves.

 *One of the most difficult things to give away is kindness, for it usually is returned.*

# Peer Pressure

*"C'mon, what's wrong with you? Live a little."*

*"Everybody's gonna be there. Let's go."*

*"Hey, we won't get caught. No one will ever know."*

*"What? Are you chicken? Try it. You'll like it."*

Do the above statements sound familiar? They should. You've probably heard them and others like them from your peers – the people your age who are your friends, classmates, or acquaintances. Statements like these are just one way peer pressure is applied. The trick is to make you feel that you will be left out and made fun of if you don't go along with the crowd. It's a form of emotional blackmail. In other words, you might feel that you have to do something or risk losing all the good things your peer group can offer.

Do you need a peer group? Sure you do. All of us need acceptance and recognition. We need the support of friends and acquaintances. There is a sense of comfort and belonging. Those are the benefits of feeling wanted and liked.

But a peer group can be negative, too. How do you know when peer pressure is negative? Sometimes that's a tough call. Part of the confusion stems from the fact that teenagers are in the "in-between" years. You're so close to being an adult, but you're not. And you're no longer a child. Sometimes you want answers and help from your parents, but you also want to be independent. It's not easy to know exactly how the pieces of the puzzle fit.

The challenge is to find a way to gain acceptance from your peers and still live up to your parents' expectations. That means using all of your experiences and knowledge, mixing them together, and making your own decisions.

There are two types of peer pressure – positive and negative. Peer pressure is not all bad. For example, having friends who urge you to try harder in school or sports can give you a good jump-start when you're not doing your best. Friends can keep you from slacking off on your responsibilities and help you when you're down. They can get you motivated and headed in the right direction. Many kids have stopped such self-destructive behaviors as drinking, drug use, and even suicide because a caring peer group stepped in. That's positive peer pressure, and it shouldn't be overlooked or underestimated.

Unfortunately, peer pressure often slides in from another angle. Things that are bad for you can be attractive, and the group can make those things sound pretty good. There is the added worry that kids won't like you or will think you're out of it or weird.

It's unfortunate, but sometimes adults aren't much help. Some of them oversimplify the problems you face. A big event in your life may seem small or foolish to them. Maybe they have forgotten how much pressure there is to go along with the group, or how intense feelings can be the first time you experience them. Adults have no doubt given you cut-and-dried answers to your problems at times. Have you ever heard statements like these?

"Don't worry about it."

"Grow up."

"Just shake it off."

"Quit acting like a baby."

"It's no big deal. You'll get over it."

"You want to know about problems? I had problems. When I was a kid...."

And of course you have heard the phrase, "Just say 'no'" many times. It's one of the catch phrases of your generation. And while it's a very good idea, it's not quite that easy to pull off. Many teen problems are just too complex to be handled with a simple response. For example, how many kids do you run around with who will immediately accept "no" for an answer when they want you to go along with them? How many say, "Oh, that's really a wise choice. You did a good job thinking that out. You should be proud of yourself." Not many, right? If you're like most people, you're going to be pestered and badgered to go along with the crowd.

When pressure is coming from friends or people you want to be friends with, it is difficult to resist. Peer groups are powerful and they can apply tremendous pressure on you to follow. After all, no one wants to be made fun of or left out. But there are times when "no" is exactly the response you should give. That takes a lot of courage and strength.

▼
• *The oldest, shortest words – "Yes" and "No" – are those which require the most thought.*

##  Jason's Story

*Jason got along with just about everyone in his class. He went to a big high school and was a starter on the soccer and golf teams. He didn't do a lot of wild things but went to the school functions and some parties. He certainly wasn't known as a "party guy" because he avoided alcohol and drugs like the plague. Occasionally, he was kidded about being a "goody two-shoes," but he handled it well and many of the kids admired his self-confidence. He had a great sense of humor, and whenever someone would tease him, Jason usually had a funny comeback.*

*Jason had deep-seated negative feelings about drinking and the pain it caused. His uncle was an alcoholic and the memories of seeing him drunk, throwing up or passed out, sometimes lying in his own vomit, were vivid in Jason's mind. Jason knew it was tearing his uncle's family apart and that hurt him terribly. He really liked his cousins; when they were kids they used to play together all the time. After his cousins reached high school, they fell in with a group of kids who frequently got drunk and had wild parties. It was well known that they had trashed one girl's house and had been in fights with kids from a neighboring school.*

*One night, Jason was at a local hangout. One of his cousins, Willie, was there also. It was evident that Willie had been drinking. He was loud and crude and seemed to love the attention he was getting. Finally, the manager came. Willie cursed at the guy and stormed out the door. He knew a* kid who was having a party so he decided to go there. On the way out, he grabbed Jason's arm and pleaded with him to come along.

At first, Jason refused. But Willie kept after him and pretty soon was making a scene in the parking lot. Willie kept talking about how close they used to be, how they were family, and how families had to stick together. It made Jason feel guilty about not doing more with his cousins.

Jason knew the kid who was having the party and he was pretty cool, not wild or anything. The kid's house wasn't too far away, so he finally told Willie that he would go with him. Jason thought that once they got there, he could always get a ride home with someone else.

As Jason was getting into Willie's car, he saw a blanket covering up something in the back seat. He asked Willie what it was; Willie smiled and said, "A case of beer, man. How cool is that?"

Jason said, "Wait a minute, I'm outta here. You're going to get busted. And I'm not going with you." Jason started to get out, but Willie begged him to go along, to at least ride to the party with his "cuz." Willie also said, "C'mon Jason. What's the big deal? You ain't drinking, man, you can't get in any trouble."

*Even though he still thought it was a bad idea, Jason gave in.*

*They never reached the party. Willie immediately floored his old Mustang and screeched out of the parking lot. Soon he was doing 60 miles an hour in a 45 mph zone. Jason pleaded with him to slow down, but Willie looked like a man possessed, staring out at the road with glassy eyes, almost like he was in a trance. Jason saw the lights flashing behind them. He told Willie to stop, but Willie took the ramp to the expressway instead.*

*The next ten minutes seemed like a ride through hell. The state trooper finally caught up with them, and Willie pulled over. The trooper had clocked the car at 90 miles an hour. He also discovered the beer in the back seat. Both kids had to take an alcohol-breath test. Even though Jason hadn't been drinking, the trooper ticketed him for being a minor in possession of alcohol. Jason knew Willie was going to be in big trouble, but asked the trooper why he was given a ticket, too. The officer sarcastically said, "It's the law, son. You're under age, and there is beer in the car. What were you going to do with it? Throw it away? Give it to needy drunks?"*

*Jason thought it was extremely unfair, but at that point, he was just glad to be alive. He had to call his parents from the police station and explain what happened. They were upset, but like Jason, they were happy that he was safe and not lying in a twisted wreck. They figured that when they appeared in court and explained what happened, the judge would understand.*

*They were wrong. Jason was found guilty. The judge said that there was beer in the car and even though Jason hadn't been drinking, he had broken the law. The judge brought up the fact that the community was cracking down on teenagers and drinking, and said Jason was in the wrong place at the wrong time. He put Jason on probation for six months and ordered him to take a drug education class. Jason was suspended from the golf team; that was a team rule. The "minor in possession" conviction would stay on his record.*

Jason knew it was poor judgment to go with his cousin, but he went anyway. Riding with someone who was drinking, having beer in the car, being involved in a high-speed chase, being charged in court, getting kicked off the golf team – all those things happened because he gave in to peer pressure. Jason knew that not going along with his cousin was the right thing to do. There's no doubt that he was punished, possibly unfairly, for his cousin's illegal behavior. But Jason also suffered for making the mistake of not sticking with what he knew was right. It was a hard lesson to learn.

**!** *There is often a difference between good sound reason and reasons that sound good.*

The very first thing you should do when kids are trying to talk you into doing something is think. Too many times, kids get into trouble by just going along with the crowd. Your generation is no different from any generation before you. There is something about the teenage years that make kids think they are invincible, that nothing can hurt them. And to many teenagers, the worst four-letter word adults can say is "don't."

Here's a list of suggestions that might help:

**1** **Think about what the group is asking you to do.** Is it wrong? Is it illegal? Why are you tempted to go along? Is it status? Are you afraid to "lose face?" Are you too weak to stand up and say, "I think this is wrong"? Do you know these people well enough to trust them?

If you have an uneasy feeling in your stomach, something is probably wrong. Use the skills of looking and listening. If a group of kids is talking about surrounding a carload of kids from another school in a parking lot, it's probably not because they're going to invite them to a picnic. Regardless of what they tell you, don't act on impulse. Think about the real message behind their words.

And think about your motivation. If you rely too much on the group for emotional support and acceptance, it's likely that you will give in to peer pressure. If you're always looking for approval from your friends and are afraid to stand up for yourself, it's likely that you will be easily influenced by what they say.

**2** **Think about what could happen.** It's difficult to think about negative consequences when a friend is raving about how much fun you're going to have. It's also hard to put up with the sarcasm and put-downs that saying "no" can trigger. Other kids can be relentless when they want to goad you into going along.

That's a good time to stop and think about what could happen. Ignore all the statements like, "Hey, everybody does it. What's wrong with you?" or "There's no way we will get caught." Those aren't good reasons to go along. Think of what could happen to you or your reputation. You have to make a promise to yourself to do not only what's legally right, but also what's morally right. Your conscience can be the biggest consequence of all. Stick to your values. If you know you're going to worry about what you did, say "no" right away. A few minutes or hours of "fun" can lead to countless days, even years, of trouble. Make a good decision and you'll feel a lot better about yourself.

▼
●
*The measure of a person's real character is what he would do if he knew he would never get caught.*

**3** **Decide beforehand what you're going to do or say.** You can sometimes predict when you might be pressured to do something. You know what's going on in your school. You know who is doing what. And you know the kids you shouldn't hang around with. Get out of situations in which you know you could be pressured.

Other situations are not so predictable. They happen because somebody comes up with a spur-of-the-moment idea and you're expected to give an immediate answer. Even then, you can have a valid reason for not going along. Think ahead about how you can respond so that you stay out of trouble. If you don't have something in mind to say, you're likely to give in. This is one time when it's okay to think of yourself instead of others.

**4** **Think of your options.** Basically, there are four things you can do.

✔ Say "yes."
✔ Say "no."
✔ Compromise.
✔ Delay.

**Say "yes"** – This is without a doubt the easiest answer to give. But often it's also the worst. If you haven't taken the time to think things through, you could be making a big mistake.

**Say "no"** – On the other hand, this is the hardest answer to give, but one that may be the best for you. There are some decisions that you don't even have to hesitate about. When your friends tell you there's a keg party, or that they're going to mess up some kids from another school, or that they're going to do something that's destructive, harmful, or illegal, then your answer should be automatic: "No" is the only right answer.

When you decide that "no" is the best answer, the hard part is sticking with it. You will have to be assertive whenever you refuse to go along. Let your friends know you mean what you say. If you have a good reason, give it. Usually, a good reason is one that involves some type of responsibility! For example, "I have to be home on time." "I promised Dad I'd mow the lawn." "My family's going out to eat tonight." "My parents would ground me for a year if they found out." Just because it doesn't sound like fun to most of the group doesn't mean it isn't a good reason.

And even if you give a good reason, it doesn't mean that other kids will accept it right away. Some people will try to keep the pressure on.

There are ways to turn them down without turning them off: You can thank them for asking you, tell them you appreciate their friendship, tell them you hope they have a good time, or empathize with whatever their problem is. But when you realize that a refusal is necessary, just say "no." Stick with what you know is right – calmly, firmly, and finally.

**Compromise** – When someone suggests doing something you're concerned about, you might be able to come up with an option that isn't as risky. You could say, for example, "Why don't we go see a movie instead?" Compromise is a "best-of-both-worlds" situation. You can still be with the group, but not join a harmful activity. It doesn't always work, but it's worth a try. Maybe you can help your friends look at situations more carefully.

Compromise requires the ability to think through and solve problems. Practice your ability to analyze problems and come up with reasonable alternatives.

**Delay** – Maybe you can wait until you see what unfolds. Saying things like, "I might be there later," or "I'll catch up with you in a little while," gives you a chance to sort through the others' real intentions and helps you think more clearly about what you've been asked to do.

Remember: You always have options. You shouldn't be forced to do anything that is illegal, immoral, or harmful to others in order to gain acceptance or respect. "No" is sometimes the only right answer, and it should jump out of your mouth. Other decisions require some thought. That's when you should give yourself time to think. A quick decision may be something you will regret later. Think things through before you make a decision, and you're more likely to make a good one.

If you haven't already faced the lure of another teenager wanting you to do something "exciting" – which usually means dangerous, harmful, or illegal – you probably will. Kids will try to get you to do something you shouldn't. And they will be very convincing. You may think you're not strong enough to resist their pressure. But you can be as strong as you want to be.

▼ *Our strength is shown in the things we stand for.*
● *Our weakness is shown in the things we fall for.*

**5** **Stick to your values and morals.** Don't compromise the good things you believe in. More important, let other people know exactly what they are. There will be times when you will be tempted to do something wrong. You might think it's worth the risk because doing it can provide immediate pleasure or popularity. But you need to think about what will happen over time. Not only are there external consequences, like getting in trouble at school, at home, or with the police, but there are internal consequences as well. In other words, there are some things you shouldn't do just because they're wrong. If you give in, you have to live with the guilt or shame of having done something you shouldn't have.

When kids try to change the good things you believe in, you have to stand up for yourself. Hold on to the values and morals your family has passed on to you. Keep your church's values and morals and your commitment to God. Don't let anybody sweet-talk or pressure you out of them.

! *Feed your faith and your doubts will starve to death.*

**6 Talk with close friends.** Express your feelings to your friends. Tell them how you wanted to give in to the pressure and how hard it was to resist. They can help. They probably have been in similar situations. Did they do the right thing? What did they learn from their experience?

**7 Trust your instincts.** If you feel uncomfortable, something is probably wrong. Tell whomever you're with to cool it for awhile until you can figure out what you're feeling. Stick to the boundaries you have set for yourself.

**❗** *It's better to sleep on what you intend doing than to stay awake over what you have done.*

**8 Be assertive.** Learn how to express your ideas and feelings without blowing up or giving in. If you are in a situation that could be harmful to you, learn how to stand your ground firmly and convincingly. Learn how to get out of negative situations (or avoid them altogether). Sometimes the answer isn't always "yes" or "no." It might be "maybe later," "Let me think about it," or "I'll wait and see."

**9 Talk to your mom or dad.** Let them know what's going on in your life. Tell them the good things that happened or the problems you encountered. Some teens are afraid of what their parents' reactions might be. And sometimes there are good reasons why they feel that way. But most parents want to know where you went and what you did because they really care.

If you have trouble talking calmly to your parents, now is the time to learn how. Learn to talk in a mature and unemotional way. Don't allow yourself to get upset when they ask questions or give you some advice. Keep your cool. That's the only mature way to proceed.

Now could be the time to change some things in their behavior, too. If they get upset when you tell them the truth, you have to train them to stay calm. Yes, that's right. It can be done. Reason with them. Set an example for them. It may not work the first time, so don't expect too much right away. But you have the power and ability to change their behavior and create a new adult relationship with them. This takes effort on your part, but it can be wonderful when it happens!

Tell them you want them to see into your world but do not want them to jump in and solve all of your problems. Let them know you will accept their advice and counsel, but you want to handle problems on your own. Assure them that if things get too tough, or if you can't handle a problem, you will come to them for help.

You may find that your parents understand and are able to help more than you think. Sharing your world with your parents can help you overcome some of the obstacles. Parents face peer pressure, too. And they have made mistakes. Their experiences can help you learn how to deal with the pressures you face.

**10** **Talk to a trusted adult.** Maybe you don't think you know an adult you can trust. Well, they're out there. Don't be afraid to ask for help. There has to be an aunt or uncle, grandparent, cousin, counselor, teacher, coach, or someone else with whom you can build a trusting relationship. There are times when you may feel powerless and when you just want some outside advice. An adult may come up with solutions you didn't consider.

You should not be forced to do something you know is wrong. There will be conflict and confusion at times. Friends (or people you thought were friends) may put more pressure on you later, say sarcastic or nasty things, or try to make you feel out of it. Figure out how you're going to respond to these people and their reasoning, and then follow through. True friends will understand.

 *If you can't find anything nice to say about your friends, maybe you have the wrong friends.*

# Teen Sex

Do you know what a minefield is? It's an innocent-looking piece of land that seems safe to walk across. But if you step in the wrong place, a land mine hidden under the ground explodes, causing injury or destruction. In teenage lives, there are many minefields. One of them involves having sex.

Many teenagers are aware of the obvious dangers of having sex. Two huge fears come to mind immediately: AIDS and pregnancy. These fears are very real, and the statistics are staggering. Kids are giving birth to kids. Kids are contracting AIDS (and other transmittable diseases) from being sexually active. We can't ignore the facts. These are very big problems.

Most of these dangers are discussed in school classrooms, broadcast on the news, or written about in magazines and newspapers. However, all of this negative information hasn't done much to deter some teenagers from having sex.

121

Why? One reason is many kids can't relate to the dangers discussed in classrooms and written about in books. It is a foreign subject to them if they haven't known or lived around other teens who have been pregnant or contracted AIDS. And statistics tend to bore most people if they can't actually see how the figures affect them. It's like talking about wars or plagues or other tragedies: You can understand a little bit and you can remember events that happened, but you don't have the intense feelings that someone who has experienced the event has.

There also is the "it-won't-happen-to-me" attitude. Scare tactics will not stop people who aren't truly afraid, no matter what anyone tells them. Many teenagers think that bad things happen to other people, not them. Unfortunately, bad things can happen to anybody.

Another reason teens become sexually active is basic curiosity. Every person who has gone through puberty has had the same curiosity. Sex is an undiscovered and mysterious land for most teenagers. They've heard about it, they've read about it, but few know exactly what it's all about.

▼ *Forbidden fruit is responsible for many a bad jam.*

The messages you receive about sex are sometimes hard to understand; many are even contradictory. Those messages can create an emotional tug-of-war in anyone's mind. On one hand, you get messages – especially from the media – which portray sex as a crucial part of life. To be full and complete, you must experience all of the joys of sex. On the other hand, you are told – especially by adults you know – not to have sex because you could die of AIDS, or contract some other disease, or get pregnant. Those images are worlds apart. You get one image of excitement and pleasure, another of fear and evil. Sexuality is very confusing.

There's no doubt about it: Sex is one of the most controversial, misunderstood, and neglected issues that teenagers face today. Some teenagers feel pressure from their dates to have sex. Some are teased if they are virgins. Rather than sticking with their own morals and values, they may choose to have sex so they're looked at as "worldly" or "mature," and not viewed as some kind of puritan freak.

Sexuality is an area where you need some straight answers from a trusted adult. The words on these pages certainly won't answer all of your questions; they are here only to give you something to think about. Face-to-face communication is the best way to get answers to the questions that really concern you.

This chapter won't dwell on the obvious physical dangers of having sex. That's not to say that they aren't real or that you shouldn't worry about them. You should. There are many statistics and loads of information that prove how risky it is to have sex at a young age. Information about sexually transmitted diseases, AIDS, and teen pregnancies is available to you if you are interested in finding out more. Your school or public library would be a good place to start.

This chapter refers to teen sex as a minefield because this decision can have devastating emotional consequences. Thousands of teenagers have suffered emotionally – more than they could ever have imagined – because they chose to be sexually active. Some lost their sense of self-worth and self-respect. And some lied to themselves to hide the truth and cover up their true feelings.

**!** *The most painful wound is a stab of conscience.*

Teens give a variety of reasons for having engaged in sex. Some wanted the status that seemed to be attached to it. Some were drunk or stoned. Some were just curious. Some felt that if they didn't have sex, a relationship would end. Others admitted they got so "carried away" that they couldn't stop. But one thing was obvious: They didn't know what they were getting themselves into. Rarely did they remember the few minutes that it took for the sex act itself. Those details were soon forgotten. What they did remember was the emotional pain – the problems and heartaches – that followed. For some, those problems occurred right away; for others, the problems crept up on them. Some of these teens got diseases. Others got pregnant. But all of them said they didn't have any idea that their lives would become so complicated and emotionally explosive because they chose to have sex.

## Monica's Story

*Monica was thrilled that Bobby had said "hi" to her in the school hallway. They were in the same history class but he sat four rows from her, so they rarely talked unless they had an in-class assignment and were in the same group. She thought he was an absolute doll. He was good-looking and athletic. All the girls thought he would be the ideal boyfriend. Who could ask for anything more?*

*That first greeting was an ice-breaker. Monica got up the nerve to talk with Bobby after class. They hit it off right away. They laughed and found out they liked a lot of the same things. Monica's heart was pounding. She thought, "Maybe he's the one. Maybe this is the guy I'm going to fall in love with."*

## What's Right for Me?

They talked a lot in school and began dating
on November 1. Monica would never forget that
day. She drew a big red heart over that date on
her calendar and in her diary.

At first, Bobby didn't try anything sexual. But
the more they dated, and the more they kissed and
hugged, the more he tried to talk her into having
sex. She refused each time and each time he would
get mad, then quiet. Many times he dropped her
off without saying goodnight. She hated the fact
that he wouldn't respect her refusal to have sex.
She wanted to wait for marriage.

Bobby's friends continually asked him if he
and Monica were "doing it." At first, it didn't
bother him to tell them the truth: No, they weren't
doing it. But the more they pressured and badgered him, the more he wanted to avoid the questions. Some of the guys were saying things like,
"What's the matter? Equipment not working?" or
"Geez, what's wrong with you? You've been going
out with her for months!"

The razzing the guys gave Bobby made him
more determined than ever to find a way to convince Monica to have sex. "What's the big deal,
anyway?" he thought. That night he again tried
to get Monica to go all the way. Again she refused.
He lost his temper. He called her filthy names
and said she wasn't a "real woman" because she
didn't want to please her man.

*Tears poured from Monica's eyes. She was so confused about the whole thing. Why did everything have to be so complicated? She knew it must be her fault. After all, some of the other girls she knew had sex with their boyfriends. Why did she think she was so special? "Dating Bobby is good for me," she thought. "I've gone to more parties, gotten to know more kids, and done more things than I've ever done before. I'm popular now. And it's because of Bobby." She finally convinced herself that she was going to do it; she was going to do whatever he wanted.*

*The next day, Monica saw Bobby with Angela. He was flirting with her, and Angela loved the attention. She kept rubbing up against Bobby and whispering something in his ear; then both of them would laugh. Monica was devastated. Angela would sleep with anybody! Everybody knew that. Monica's friends asked her what was going on, but she couldn't answer. Her heart was in her throat, and she knew she would burst into tears if she tried to say anything.*

*The rest of the school day was torture. The thought of Bobby with Angela burned in her mind. "He's going to have sex with her just to get back at me," she thought. Then she cursed herself for being so prudish. No, not prudish, just plain stupid! She was frantic. She had to talk to Bobby before the end of the school day.*

*She caught up with him by his locker. He had this weird smile on his face that irritated and worried her at the same time. She asked him what was going on with Angela. "Just talking," he replied. Then he added, "For now, anyway." She asked what that meant, but he just kept saying sarcastically, "What do you think's going to happen?" She pleaded with him not to be around Angela. She said she would go out with him that night and give him anything he wanted, but he had to promise to drop Angela right away. He smiled that same smile and said he would.*

*Monica was scared. She worried about what having sex would be like, about getting some disease, about getting pregnant. She countered all of those worries with the belief that if she didn't please Bobby, she would lose him. That's all that really mattered now.*

*When he picked her up, she asked if he could get some alcohol. Bobby was amazed; Monica never wanted to drink. "This is too much," he chuckled to himself. He wondered what she would be like with a little booze in her. "Maybe she'll lighten up a little bit," he thought.*

*It wasn't any trouble getting something to drink. Bobby knew a guy that could always get it for him. He bought a bottle of peppermint schnapps. He gave the bottle to Monica, and she* took a slug. She hated the minty, thick taste but kept drinking it anyway. She just wanted to relax.

Bobby was rough. It was obvious that he was only using her to satisfy himself. She didn't even feel most of what was happening. Her body and mind were numb. She remembered it was like the time the dentist gave her a shot of painkiller – she knew what was happening but there was no feeling at all.

There were no loving emotions. There was no romance. It wasn't the way she expected it. She wished she hadn't gotten into this mess. She worried about her reputation. The schnapps was making her sick. She felt like vomiting. She just wanted to go home and be alone.

The next day, Bobby acted like a conquering hero. Guys were giving him "high fives" and raising their arms like they were signaling for a touchdown. Everyone knew he had scored. Watching him prance like a rooster made her feel so small, so insignificant. What had she done?

One girl came up to Monica and asked, "So, you finally did it, huh? Was he good?" Other girls asked similar questions. "It's none of your business," she thought, and at that time she really wanted to run away and hide. She wanted to scream and tell all of them to get away. This wasn't the way it was supposed to be. This wasn't a game. Why wouldn't people leave her alone?

*Bobby and Monica went out a few more times, but their relationship was never the same. Bobby only wanted sex. Because they had done it once, he thought he had a green light to go ahead anytime they were together. Monica felt guilty and used, mad and revengeful. The negative feelings she had toward Bobby grew like a cancer. She wondered what she ever saw in him and why she was so foolish to give up everything she believed in. She had promised herself that she would remain a virgin until she was married. She made that vow in church, and she broke it. She thought she was in love, and she wasn't. She made a mistake, and now everyone knew about it. Some of her old friends avoided her, and guys she liked didn't talk to her much anymore.*

*Monica felt like trash. She felt stained and worthless. She thought about hurting or even killing herself to end the pain.*

*After she broke up with Bobby, he began spreading rumors about how "hot" she was and how many times they had "done the nasty." He was telling lies, but everyone believed what he said. His friends called her for dates and asked her to go to parties. One guy even said he wanted to date an "experienced" woman for a change. Monica cringed every time the phone rang. She didn't date again for a long time. It was just too much to bear.*

Did Monica get a disease? No. Did she get pregnant? No. Did she suffer emotionally? Yes.

Many teens who become sexually active don't realize all the complexities and consequences of their actions, emotional as well as physical. They aren't ready to shoulder the responsibilities that having sex demands. Monica, for example, made a big decision for all the wrong reasons. She didn't stick with the promise she had made to herself. Maybe worst of all, she damaged her own self-worth. She didn't like herself and hated what she had done; she didn't even like looking in the mirror. It was difficult for Monica to forgive herself.

 *It is not easy to find happiness in ourselves, and it is not possible to find it elsewhere.*

## Why Take the Risk?

Let's look at other reasons why some teens risk crossing the minefield of sex. Teenagers are at an "almost" age. They're almost old enough to be an adult. That means they're right on the verge of being independent. That's exciting, but it leads to impatience. Most teenagers don't want to wait too long for anything. Our society is fast. Fast food. Instant cash. Immediate gratification. In the rush to become adults, some teenagers want to do "adult" things. They think, "If adults can do it, why can't I?" Having sex is viewed as adult behavior. So, to be an adult, you have to have sex. That's a confused and convoluted message, but many teens believe it.

Some teens are unhappy with their lives. They want some sense of who they are. Some want to please others or to feel wanted and cared for. In a confused search to solve problems, they think having sex is the solution.

Another reason teenagers feel confused about sex concerns the type of messages they receive and where they get their advice. Whom do you go to for answers? Many teens get their information (or misinformation) from their friends, and rarely talk directly with a trusted adult about sexual matters.

 *If God had believed in permissiveness, He would have given us the Ten Suggestions.*

And your generation is bombarded with messages about sex in movies, songs, TV shows, and magazines. Let's be honest here. Sex sells. It always has. Anyone out to make a buck just spices up their product with something sexy, and Presto! Instant success. You can consciously disregard these messages, but if you hear them enough, they will affect your thinking and behavior. That's an old brainwashing technique.

Think about how sex is portrayed in some movies, music videos, and TV shows. Sex is exciting and fun, adventurous and stimulating. Those people (actors) are just having a good time; rarely does anyone suffer emotionally or physically. It's just fun, so they do it. That's a bunch of garbage. Sex is not a sporting event. There's more to it than the physical act itself, although there are some people who believe that's all it is. There are many guys who make a "game" of seeing how often they can score. The same rings true for some girls.

Some kids are so bombarded by messages to have sex that it's no wonder they believe it's the most important thing in a relationship. They're told they're "out of it" if they're not sexually active. The messages follow simple equations and basic math: Dates = sex. Boy + girl = sex. Sorry, wrong answer. Check your addition.

 *Dating isn't the same as mating. Just because the body is ready doesn't mean the mind is.*

Here are some messages teenagers see and hear about sex. Take some time to check out how often and where you hear these messages. Boys are being taught that:

✔ Having sex is the primary reason to go out with girls.

133

✔ Their role as a male is to fulfill a girl's sexual urges.

✔ Girls are nothing but sex objects who are there to provide what boys need and want.

✔ They need to be aggressive in order to obtain sex. The message is, "If you don't get laid, you're not a man."

✔ They need to "sweet talk" and play word games with girls to get them in sexual situations.

✔ It's all right for a relationship with a girl to involve seduction or force.

Girls are being taught that:

✔ They have to be attractive and seductive. Attractiveness has only one purpose: to sexually excite boys.

✔ They should give sex and really want it.

✔ They need to give sex to be real women.

✔ Giving sex is the only way they can get the attention they want and need.

None of these things has anything to do with love or respect. These messages have one thing in common: One person wants something and uses another person to get it. But using someone is not part of loving someone. In fact, they are opposites.

Then there's the old double standard. Guys want to have sex with girls but don't necessarily want to marry someone who's "easy." The same guy who did the sweet-talking to score the night before might not even look at the girl the next day at school.

So now, let's put all of this in perspective. Let's talk straight. Girls are not put on this earth to be sexual objects. Guys are not just walking hormones whose only purpose is to have sex with girls. That is sex reduced to its lowest form.

Give yourself some credit. You're not a pawn in a sexual chess game. People don't control your behavior or make decisions for you. If everyone else is "doing it," that doesn't mean you have to. It's up to you to make wise choices, moral choices – the kinds of choices you can live with.

Don't confuse sex with love. Don't confuse friendship with popularity. They are different things entirely. You have to realize how much of your life is on the line when it comes to sexual behavior. You have to protect yourself – your body, mind, and self-esteem – because there are a lot of people who will try to use you. Don't allow yourself to be used. Stand up for what you know is morally right.

## When Will You Be Ready?

There will come a time when you are ready to enter into a satisfying, loving adult relationship with someone. You should look forward with excitement to the time when you will marry someone and start a family. In that relationship, you can explore your sexuality and share intimacy with someone you love. You will be fully ready to commit yourself to becoming a good husband or wife and a good mom or dad. That's a special, wonderful time in your life and something that's definitely worth waiting for.

 *Someone to love, something good to do, and something to look forward to – these are the ingredients of a happy life.*

Before that time comes, you can have a loving, affectionate relationship without sex. Happy relationships include working together, helping one another, sharing opinions and dreams, and having fun. You can be romantic without being sexual. You can be affectionate without being sexual. In fact, most long-lasting relationships between men and women start with friendship, not with sexuality. You don't need sex to feel like an adult, to feel accepted by someone you care about. You don't need to prove your love by using your body.

Sex involves responsibility. It involves self-control. True sexuality is more than just "doing it." Sex is not a game. And having sex before you're married and emotionally ready to commit yourself to one person in a loving relationship is a decision that will have a negative effect on the rest of your life. There's a lot at stake, and the odds are stacked against you.

We've discussed many aspects of sex and the choices teens have to make about it. We hope these issues have raised questions in your mind about the biological and emotional consequences of teen sexuality. This book doesn't have all the answers. To get more information, we suggest you do the following:

**1** **Talk with someone who is trustworthy and mature enough to give you good advice.** How do you know if someone is trustworthy? A trustworthy person is one who shares your faith and morals, not someone who wants to separate you from positive family values. A mature person is someone you can share your feelings with, someone who won't just tell you what you want to hear, but what you need to hear. Try your parents first. If you're fortunate enough to have an open relationship with your parents and feel comfortable talking to them about sexual matters, that's a great situation – you should feel very fortunate and loved.

If it's impossible to talk with your parents about such personal things, please find another adult – someone older and wiser, someone trustworthy and responsible – who can give you straightforward answers. An older brother or sister, an aunt or uncle, or a cousin may be a good resource. Other options may be your youth minister, pastor or priest, counselor, or doctor. Don't be afraid to ask questions. That's how you learn.

**2** **Find out more about relationships.** There are many other books on the market that talk about both the negative and positive aspects of relationships, especially about how we should treat members of the opposite sex. Don't rely only on what you see and hear around you. In other words, ask questions, read books, and listen to experts. Talk to adults who have experienced rich, rewarding relationships, and learn from them.

One of the most important ways to have a good relationship with someone of the opposite sex is to have the ability to make friends. Concentrate on learning and practicing other skills such as sensitivity to others, helpfulness, empathy, and tolerance.

Another relationship that you should never forget is your relationship with God. Prayer should be a constant in your life, but it especially helps you in times when you feel you have nowhere to turn or you're worried about making the wrong decision. Stick with your spiritual values. If you can feel good about yourself, then you probably made a wise decision.

**3** **Read about emotional, sexual, and physical development.** Know what is happening to your feelings, mind, and body. Some teenagers find it hard to cope with the changes taking place during puberty. They feel frightened, confused, or stressed.

Hormones are racing through your body, and they change the way you feel. Education can relieve some of the worry or confusion caused by all the physical and emotional changes.

Know the proper terms for genitalia and the human reproductive system. There are hundreds of slang terms for these, but your goal is to have an adult discussion, so don't reduce it to slang. It will turn off most adults right away because they have attached "dirty" thoughts to those words. Slang also will make most adults defensive from the beginning. Do your homework; know the proper terms.

**4** **Find out about AIDS and sexually transmitted diseases.** There seems to be a new disease for every generation. Know what can happen to sexually active people. Find out about teenage pregnancies and abortions. Take these things seriously.

**5** **Read about how pregnancy occurs – what really happens during the miracle of conception.** Many teenage pregnancies can be traced to lack of knowledge. You need to know the truth about pregnancies. Read about the growth of the baby in a mother's womb. This isn't like buying a new doll to have someone to play with. This is real. Being a mother or father carries a load of responsibility.

The more you know about the kinds of risks involved with sex, the better you will feel about making a decision to abstain.

You will find that having sex can wait. You don't have to wander aimlessly into the minefield. Treat your mind and your body with respect.

The right person is out there. The right time will come. But it's not now. Wait.

# Con Artists

Has someone ever conned you? Has someone you liked fairly well, and even trusted a little, ever talked you into doing something wrong? Just about everyone, at least once, has been fooled by someone.

Words are powerful. There are some people who are masters at talking other people into doing something they shouldn't. Con artists trick and manipulate others by what they say and do.

This is different than peer pressure where a group of people tries to get you to go along with them. A con artist is one person, and he or she purposely tries to get you to do something wrong. Usually, the person is older and more "experienced." He's learned what makes people tick, and he takes advantage of that knowledge in order to get what he wants.

Think of a con artist as a fisherman. The fisherman uses lures to attract the fish to his hook.

Or he uses bait that looks like the real deal. A fish swims around with his mouth watering, thinking of the feast before him. He is a little cautious at first, but everything looks so good that he finally takes the bait. Wham! The fisherman sets the hook. His "act" convinced the fish to bite. He controls it now. He made everything look so good that the fish couldn't resist.

Get the picture? That's basically what a con artist does to his victim.

Con artists play word games. We call them "language cons." That's part of his bait. Once he finds something a person will fall for – some weakness or need – he exploits and manipulates that weakness. Then all he has to do is play his victim like a fish on a line and reel him or her in. Con artists really don't care what happens to someone else as long as they get what they want.

Note: The con artist will be referred to as "he," but that's only for easier reading. A con artist can be female or male.

 *There are three types of people: right-handed, left-handed, and under-handed.*

Language cons are used for many reasons and in different ways. Someone may try to talk you out of your money, convince you to steal something, make you hurt someone else, or convince you to have sex. Language cons sound good. Bad motives come gift-wrapped in pretty words.

## Who Gets Tricked?

Anyone can fall prey to a con artist under the right circumstances. Most likely are people who fit into one or more of the following categories:

✔ Young and inexperienced in relationships

✔ Timid or shy

✔ Desperate for someone to love and take care of them

✔ Overly trusting

✔ Unable to solve problems on their own

Why are these people targets of con games? Because they are looking for someone to help them feel safe and protected. They want to believe there is someone who can make their lives better. In truth, they're looking for someone to depend on, either to feel better about themselves or to give them something they couldn't get on their own.

Young people are often easy prey for scheming adult con artists. Many cases of child abuse start when an unsuspecting young person blindly does what an adult asks. The con artist is very convincing; whatever he says, the child believes. The young child just doesn't know any better.

But young people aren't the only ones who become victims of a con artist. Teenagers and adults often fall into the same traps.

## The Con Artist's Plan

How does a con artist persuade a victim to follow along? First of all, the con artist creates a false sense of trust. His intent is not to make you a true friend; it's to trick you. But you don't know that; he hides his real motives.

The con artist says and does things to make you believe he is honest and trusting. This could involve buying you gifts, bailing you out of trouble, protecting you from other people, or showering you with attention.

Sounds like a good friend, right? Wrong. There's a big difference between a con artist's game and true friendship. Con artists are masters at creating relationships where they can exploit someone. That means they use another person for selfish reasons – to please only themselves. And they expect to be paid back.

One of the keys to real friendship is liking a person for who he or she is, not for what they can give. Friendship is based on respect. When someone is treated like an object, like a game piece to be moved here and there, that respect vanishes. By building a false sense of trust, by making you believe that you're truly cared for, the con artist wins control over you. And control has no place in a healthy relationship.

Con artists use language cons over and over in an attempt to convince you to do something wrong. A con artist has a powerful mastery of words. That doesn't mean he has a big vocabulary; it means that when he says something, you believe it. And the more the con artist says something, the more likely you are to be persuaded. The con artist doesn't give up.

After the con artist gains some form of control over you, he uses you. The con artist has been successful at tricking people in the past and will use any sneaky ploy to gain your trust. Most people don't even realize at first that they've been tricked because they believe what the con artist says. They obey without thinking.

## ⊩ Crystal's Story

Note: The following three letters were written by a 19-year-old man to Crystal, a 12-year-old girl. When the man wrote the first letter, they had known each other for two weeks. He uses many language cons in his letters. Letters are reproduced as they appeared, with grammatical and spelling errors intact.

# Letter 1

Hi, honey. How are you? When I said I would give you something special, I take that back. I don't want you to think anything about that. I want you to do good cause hopefully you'd feel good and that would make me feel good. Speaking of good bodies, you got one yourself. I like you for what you are, not what you can give. It's just that sometimes when I'm around you, I feel like doing this and that. I want to get closer and stuff and don't do all this negative stuff. Then nature can take its time. Let's get closer but don't go too far. I want you badly. But I will wait if I have to. I have other stuff to say but I don't want to write it down.

# Letter 2

What's up my love? I have been thinking about you night and day. I've been thinking about how much I love you which is alot. Some other things I've been thinking about is when I first saw you and when I held you in my arms in back of your school. I miss you so much. I can't wait to see you again. There's alot of things I love about you. You're smart, you have a sweet personality and you are very pretty. You are very special to me. Just thinking about you makes me happy. I really want to be there for you. You are too sweet to be *taken advantage of and treated bad. And I don't want that to happen. I do like to do it, but we are going to take it nice and slow. You know what I'm saying. Some time I will show you how much I love you, but not right now. Gotta go.*

# Letter 3

*My dearest,*

*How are you doin' sweetheart? Myself, I'm takin' it E.Z. I had a lovely time with you yesterday. You really lightened my day. I want you to know that I think you are a very attractive and sweet person. But, I am a lot older than you and where I come from they call it "robbin' the cradle." You know what I'm saying. Even tho' age is just a number. So we have to be careful baby. I still like you and want to get to know you real good. If you know what I mean. I don't want any of these players up here trying to take advantage of you because you're so young. You can trust me. I want to be there for you. If anybody gets you, it better be me. You're so special to me. Write back please. Love.*

Were these typical love letters? No. Given the circumstances, this guy was making an obvious attempt to manipulate a younger and less experienced person. And he obviously used Crystal. He convinced her to sneak out at night to have sex with him. She trusted him; she looked to him for safety. The result of her trust? She ran away to be with him so often that her parents placed her in a group home. He never wrote or called her again. Did he have Crystal's best interests at heart? No way.

Once you figure out the types of games con artists play, you take away their manipulative power. It's like the script of an old vampire movie. Once the vampire is exposed to sunlight, he loses his strength. Your knowledge of the con artist's tricks is like the sunlight that destroys the vampire. Once the sun shines on the con artist's true character, he loses all his power.

In the next section, we'll talk about some ways to tell the good guys from the bad guys.

## The Con Artist's Game

In any relationship you have with others – and especially in dating relationships – watch out for several types of undesirable people. The problem is you can't identify a con artist by his looks or clothing. The good guys don't wear white hats and the bad guys don't wear black hats as in some old western movie. But all con artists have one thing in common – they play word games to get something they want. Knowing the tricks they use is one way to pick out the con artists.

Here are some lines these people use:

*"It's okay, don't worry. I know what
I'm doing."*

*"Just this once. Trust me."*

*"You know I wouldn't do anything
to hurt you."*

*"This is normal. This is the way it's
supposed to be."*

*"Prove how much you care about me."*

*"What's the big deal? Everybody does it."*

*"If you leave me, I'll kill myself."*

The con artist has many tricks up his sleeve. Here are some common tactics:

**Alcohol and Drugs.** This is one of the oldest tricks in the book – get someone drunk or stoned and they're like puppets on a string. Language cons are very convincing when your defenses are down. Not only are you likely to do something you normally wouldn't do, but the con artist also can use being drunk or stoned as an excuse for his behavior: "Don't blame me, man. I was so out of it, I didn't know what I was doing." But the con artist knew exactly what was going on.

Some kids develop problems with substance abuse. Some get hooked, and then do whatever the con artist wants in order to keep the supply of booze or drugs coming. And some use drugs to forget what they've done. So it all becomes one blurry nightmare.

It makes no difference to the con artist because he got what he wanted.

**Flattery.** Most con artists are smooth talkers. They can lay it on thick. They use flattery to convince you that you're the greatest person who ever lived – that you are the sexiest, smartest, funniest, most desirable creature God ever put on this earth. The problem is you may want to believe it! All of the attention that comes with flattery feels good.

There's one big difference between praise and flattery – praise is sincere; flattery is not. Praise shows approval or admiration for someone or something. Flattery is excessive and designed to get something. That's it in a nutshell. Once you become blinded by flattery, you can't see that you're being manipulated.

**❗** *Smart people believe half of what they hear. Smarter people know which half to believe.*

It's always wise to watch out for smooth talkers. They're real players. If they say one thing, but do the opposite, be careful. Watch what that person does around others. Listen to what that person tells others. Then you may find out if he or she is worth believing.

▼ *A flatterer is one who says things to your face*
● *that he wouldn't say behind your back.*

**Status.** Con artists usually can provide something you want, such as money, popularity, drugs, or attention. Unfortunately, to get what the con artist can give you, you have to do what he wants.

We've talked about the motives of the con artist. It's also wise to examine your own. Why are you willing to let someone control you? Do popularity or material things mean so much to you that you would do anything for or give anything to the con artist just to get them?

Do some good old-fashioned soul-searching here. Stick with what you know is morally and legally right.

**Intimidation.** Intimidation is the nasty kid brother of anger and violence. An intimidator may not actually use physical force, but he wants you to believe that he will. And the threat is real enough to frighten you.

Intimidation can stop people from doing what they should do, or frighten people into doing something they normally wouldn't do. Either way, the victim gives in to threats made by another person.

The most common form of intimidation involves someone telling you that something bad will happen to you if you don't do what that person wishes. Instead of making a scene, you give in a little. After that, the person wants more control over you. The intimidation occurs more often or becomes more severe. Eventually, you begin to feel trapped, scared, and unsure of what to do.

Intimidation often sounds something like this: "If you don't do this, I'll...," or "I'm only telling you once; you'd better do what I say or you'll be sorry." Once you believe that a person will follow through with these threats, you're likely to change the way you act.

Sometimes con artists will actually use physical force when a victim resists. Once that happens, the con artist has even more power. The victim realizes it could happen again. If you find yourself in a relationship like this, get out of it immediately. Go to an adult or close friend you can trust and get some help and advice. You probably can't handle this situation yourself.

When a con artist harasses, intimidates, or uses violence against a victim, he has committed a crime. The victim needs to seek protection, either from a trusted adult or the police. This is especially true when the victim realizes what the con artist is doing, and the con artist sees the victim as a witness against him.

**❗** *The truth may be clear as a bell, but it's not always tolled.*

**Persuasion.** Have you ever known anyone who was so convincing that it was hard not to do whatever the person asked you to do? Regardless of how hard you tried to resist, he or she always had more reasons (or reasons that sounded better) than the ones you had for saying "no."

People who are successful in winning someone over are masters of persuasion. First, they are skilled at arguing. They can give examples of why they are right and you are wrong. Second, they can attack you with an arsenal of reasons you hadn't considered. They're slick operators. Finally, they know how to beg and plead until you give in. And the reasons and arguments and begging all seem to make sense, at least for the moment. Persuasion can wear you down unless you do something to stop it.

Be cautious around someone who continually uses arguments and lots of reasons, or who pleads with you to do something, especially when you have refused to go along. Someone who doesn't respect your right to say "no" doesn't respect you. If you think someone is trying to manipulate you, firmly say "no" and stick by your decision. Don't give in.

▼
● *A lie can travel around the world and back*
*again while the truth is lacing up its sneakers.*

**Lying.** We all know what lying is. Everyone has probably fibbed occasionally or told a "little white lie." Lying is saying something that's not true but hoping that others will believe it is. It's purposeful. Whatever a person's reasons are for lying, the person means to do it. Usually, people lie to either get out of doing something or to get out of trouble.

People who use word games to trick others lie frequently. Con artists lie to get their victims to do things for them. And they really do their homework; they are very convincing and know how to spruce up their stories with all kinds of details to make them sound believable. That's why it is so important to identify a person's intentions by looking at his or her actions rather than merely listening to his or her words. If someone you know continually tells lies, be on your guard – that person wants something from you. Keep your eyes and ears open.

▼
● *Why must the phrase "It's none of my business"*
*always be followed with the word "but"?*

If you hear someone continually saying untrue or hurtful things about others, you can be pretty sure that he or she will say the same things about you when you're not around. Frequent lying is not just a bad habit; it is a bad problem. Liars are insecure and the truth scares them. Responsibility scares them. Anyone you can't rely on to be honest is not a good choice for a friend.

**!** *A lie may take care of the present, but it has no future.*

## Whom Can You Trust?

How do you cut through the double meanings and lies that go along with word games and get to the truth? How do you know whom you can believe?

Here are some things to think about:

**1** **Word games are used by people who want to take advantage of you and get their own way.** They seldom care that you could get hurt.

Think of the consequences of what the person is trying to convince you to do. Could you get in trouble? Could someone get hurt? Will you end up doing something that you have been taught is wrong? If so, that person is conning you.

155

When a person is relentless in his or her attempts to convince you, put you down, or frighten you, then you can be fairly sure this person isn't acting in your best interests.

Don't fall for the lure of fancy words. Make your own decisions and think before you act.

**2** **Be aware of a con artist's tricks.** If there is a difference between what a person says and does, there's little chance of developing a healthy relationship. If someone gives you compliments and sweet-talk to get you to do something, beware of this person's real intentions. Doing what's best for you is probably not one of them.

If you find that a person always wants something in return for favors he or she has done for you, watch out. He is keeping score in a game you shouldn't play. Friends do things for one another because they want to, not because they want something in return.

**3** **Talk with a trusted adult or close friend.** Open up to someone with whom you can be honest. Friends sometimes see things in your behavior that you don't see. And don't be afraid to talk to an adult you trust – a parent, relative, teacher, coach, clergyman, or counselor. An adult's opinion is very important when you're worried that someone is trying to take advantage of you. Listen carefully and don't get upset if you hear something you don't want to hear (like the truth). Stay calm and think about what they have said, then act on it.

**4** **Don't feel guilty.** People who use word games and language cons often will try to make you feel like you are to blame for something that happens or that you let them down. Don't buy it. They want to please themselves, not others. They'll try to make you feel bad so you'll give in and do whatever they're trying to get you to do. It's great to be sensitive to the feelings of others but you have to draw the line when someone is trying to use you.

**5** **Check with others.** If you think a person is using language cons, don't be afraid to ask questions. Do your friends know anything about this person? Have they ever been conned by him or her? Do they know what this person's close friends are like? Sooner or later, a con artist's game is going to be revealed. When it is, he or she loses the power to trick people.

**6** **Don't give in.** When you decide to say "no" to a con artist, stick with your decision. The person probably will try many different angles, hoping you'll finally give in. You have to be firm and stand your ground.

## What Should I Say?

Saying "no" is difficult, especially to someone who is skilled at using language cons. Some people are so smooth and convincing that you can momentarily fail to see what he or she really wants. It's always a good idea to have some "stock" answers for someone who's putting the pressure on you to do something wrong.

The following is a list of responses that may help you think of something to say in such situations:

✔ "If you really care, you'll understand."

✔ "I respect myself. Why can't you?"

✔ "I have too much to lose."

✔ "It's not worth it."

✔ "I want to be respected, not dejected."

✔ "It's not right. I hope you understand."

✔ "When I said 'no,' I meant it."

✔ "I know you don't agree with me, but I want you to respect my feelings."

When another person is trying to convince you to do something sexual, here are some possible responses:

✔ "You don't really want me. You want sex."

✔ "I'm not ready for sex. Don't push me into doing it."

✔ "Love is a two-way street. You only want it one way: your way."

✔ "My brain's between my ears, not my legs."

✔ "I want real love, not an imitation."

✔ "I want you to love me, not my body."

✔ "It's not worth it. Love is based on friendship, and you don't hurt friends."

✔ "I care enough about you to do what's right for both of us."

✔ "Real love isn't over in just a few minutes."

✔ "You don't own my body. And I'm certainly not renting it out!"

Okay, some of these lines may sound sarcastic and you might not want to use them. They are just examples. But the point is that it's a good idea to think ahead and have something to say to someone who tries to con you.

It's too bad you have to be this cautious. But con artists are very real. They're in every town, every school, and every neighborhood. Not only are their behaviors negative, but so are their values. It is not right to use or manipulate other people, but it's the only way con artists know. This information was not presented to scare you, although your level of paranoia has probably risen a notch or two. It was presented to help you avoid being hurt or used. You must be able to see the enemy in order to fight him (or her).

At the same time, please remember that there are some wonderful people out there who would make great friends. There are people who are loyal and honest. There are people who really do care about you and want you to be happy. Not everyone is selfish and deceitful.

Learning how to sort out the good from the bad – learning whom you can trust and whom you can't – is a skill that you will continually develop. You'll make some poor choices along the way, trust someone you shouldn't, or believe a well-contrived line or two. That's part of growing up. But if you know how to identify the con artists, you can keep yourself or someone you know from being a victim.

 *Sin has many tools, but a lie is the handle which fits them all.*